[H.A.S.C. No. 115–60]

SECURING THE PEACE AFTER THE FALL OF ISIL

HEARING

BEFORE THE

SUBCOMMITTEE ON OVERSIGHT AND INVESTIGATIONS

OF THE

COMMITTEE ON ARMED SERVICES HOUSE OF REPRESENTATIVES

ONE HUNDRED FIFTEENTH CONGRESS

FIRST SESSION

HEARING HELD
OCTOBER 3, 2017

U.S. GOVERNMENT PUBLISHING OFFICE

27–563   WASHINGTON : 2018

CONTENTS

Page

STATEMENTS PRESENTED BY MEMBERS OF CONGRESS

WITNESSES

APPENDIX

SECURING THE PEACE AFTER THE FALL OF ISIL

House of Representatives,
Committee on Armed Services,
Subcommittee on Oversight and Investigations,
Washington, DC, Tuesday, October 3, 2017.

The subcommittee met, pursuant to call, at 3:26 p.m., in room 2212, Rayburn House Office Building, Hon. Vicky Hartzler (chairwoman of the subcommittee) presiding.

OPENING STATEMENT OF HON. VICKY HARTZLER, A REPRESENTATIVE FROM MISSOURI, CHAIRWOMAN, SUBCOMMITTEE ON OVERSIGHT AND INVESTIGATIONS

Mrs. HARTZLER. Good afternoon. This hearing will come to order.

I want to welcome the ranking member who is here. Started seeing subcommittee members—we are starting a few minutes early. And I know that they will be coming in. And we want to thank all the witnesses for being here today.

So in connection with today's hearing, I want to ask for unanimous consent that any committee members who may be joining us be able to participate in the hearing with the understanding that all sitting subcommittee members will be recognized for questions prior to those not assigned to the subcommittee. So ordered, and without objection.

We convene today to consider how the United States intends to secure the peace once ISIL [Islamic State of Iraq and the Levant] is defeated. This is a very important issue to the committee, to this subcommittee, and to me, the Ranking Member Moulton, and other members. It is essential and appropriate that we exercise proper oversight as our country's plans are formulated and funding is authorized.

Following Operation Iraqi Freedom, the United States worked to reestablish civil institutions and rebuild the military and police forces in Iraq. Nonetheless, conditions in the country deteriorated, leaving a security void that ISIL managed to exploit. We owe it to our men and women in uniform to learn lessons from that experience so that history does not repeat itself.

It is critical that we do all we can here in Congress to ensure a stable Iraq after ISIL is defeated. Today's hearing will offer members an opportunity to learn more about how the administration intends to achieve success beyond the battlefield.

Our first panel of very insightful outside experts will discuss the broader strategic issues associated with ISIL's loss of territory and highlight critical issues that should be considered as the administration's Iraq policy evolves. Our second panel today will address the numerous challenges associated with stabilization and rebuild-

(1)

ing in Iraq and discuss the status of U.S. government efforts to improve the political and security environment in Iraq.

I now turn to my colleague, Ranking Member Moulton, for his in-
troductory remarks.

[The prepared statement of Mrs. Hartzler can be found in the
Appendix on page 41.]

STATEMENT OF HON. SETH MOULTON, A REPRESENTATIVE FROM MASSACHUSETTS, RANKING MEMBER, SUBCOMMITTEE ON OVERSIGHT AND INVESTIGATIONS

Mr. MOULTON. Thank you, Madam Chairwoman. And I want to
echo the comments on how fortunate we feel to have such a tal-
ented and distinguished panel here to help us understand these
problems.

Today the subcommittee will focus on the critically important
task of securing the peace in Iraq after the defeat of ISIS [Islamic
State of Iraq and Syria]. I echo Chairwoman Hartzler's frustration
at securing appropriate administration witnesses to answer the full
gamut of questions the Oversight and Investigations Subcommittee
is within its purview to raise, but I am grateful for everyone's presence here today and ongoing service to our country.

I also appreciate our outside witnesses who will bring considerable depth of expertise to bear on this subject, including Ambassador Crocker, whom I first met in Iraq while serving under General Petraeus. I think that is where I met you, as well, Ken.

As we convene here today, Iraqi security forces supported by the
U.S. advise and assist mission have succeeded in retaking most
major population centers once controlled by ISIS—Fallujah, Ramadi, and Mosul, ISIS's power center in Iraq. Most recently, coalition-
supported Iraqi forces seized back the city of Tal Afar in the northwestern corner of Iraq and only isolated ISIS strongholds remain
outside of Hawija, Qaim, and other pockets along the Syria-Iraq
border.

Such victories have not been without a human toll. ISIS's brutal
tactics, employing civilians as human shields, vehicle-borne improvised explosive devices, and booby-trapped residential areas resulted in over 1,400 Iraqi troops killed and at least 7,000 wounded,
according to our embassy in Baghdad. During the campaign, two
American service members were killed and over 20 were wounded.

The U.S. commander of the Combined Joint Task Force in charge
of the counter-ISIS campaign, Lieutenant General Stephen Townsend, called it the, quote "worst fighting he had seen in 35 years"
end quote, of combat experience and likened it to Fallujah 2004 on
steroids. Civilian losses have been greater still, with the latest
U.N. [United Nations] estimates at 8,000 killed and 1.2 million
rendered homeless, displaced by the fighting.

Despite the tragic human toll, I am encouraged by the progress
we have made in partnership with Iraqi forces to defeat the
scourge of ISIS and look forward to hearing from our witnesses an
update on the final stages of the military campaign. As important
and necessary as these operations are to militarily defeat ISIS, I
remain concerned that without sufficient post-conflict planning and
resourcing we will find ourselves and Iraqi forces condemned to re-

fighting the same battles so many have already given their lives for in the past.

At its core, what troubles Iraq are fundamentally political questions. Just as I disagreed with the Obama administration, I am again concerned that this new administration is not sufficiently prioritizing such underlying political dynamics.

What does this mean? First and foremost, I am concerned Iraqi security forces may be woefully unprepared to provide security to Iraqi civilians and ensure displaced persons can return to their homes without fear of attack or retribution. Experts I have heard here from Washington and in Iraq have expressed worries of insufficient hold forces and police, compounded by the beleaguered state of Iraqi military units, reeling from the toll of the brutal counter-ISIS campaign.

Without sufficient local security arrangements, we cannot expect for Iraq to be stabilized, for civilians to return to normalcy, and for communities to be defended against the emergence of a, quote "ISIS 2.0" or other militant groups. Moreover, without capable and professional security forces, we risk seeing a repeat of the same sectarian tensions leading to Sunni embitterment that provided fertile ground for the growth of ISIS in the first place.

Beyond the provisioning of civilian security, key gaps and problems remain to be addressed, such as acute food insecurity, insufficient access to health care, destroyed infrastructure, degraded public services and utilities, newly inflamed grievances among local communities, and insufficient plans for governance arrangements in many areas.

Both as a Marine infantry officer who worked side-by-side with Iraqis to turn the tide of the insurgency and now as a Congressman and ranking member of this Oversight and Investigations Subcommittee, I look forward to your testimony and hope to hear a proactive, whole-of-government strategy that represents the only chance of success.

I cannot tell you how painful it is as an Iraq war veteran to see us fighting and refighting the same battles we fought and for which so many of our friends gave their lives. At this rate, my children will be fighting these same battles. We must hear from this administration how this time will be different, how this time you will ensure a political resolution so that the U.S. military doesn't have to keep coming back and cleaning up the mess every time Iraqi politics falls apart.

Thank you, Chairwoman Hartzler, and I yield back.

[The prepared statement of Mr. Moulton can be found in the Appendix on page 42.]

Mrs. HARTZLER. Thank you, Mr. Moulton.

So I am pleased to recognize our witnesses we have for our first panel. They are very distinguished and we appreciate their time. We are joined by the Honorable Ryan Crocker, former Ambassador to Iraq, and currently serving as diplomat in residence in the Woodrow Wilson School at Princeton University. We have Dr. Kenneth Pollack, resident scholar at the American Enterprise Institute, and Dr. Marc Lynch, professor of political science at the Elliott School of International Affairs at The George Washington University.

So, welcome. Ambassador Crocker, we will start with your statement.

STATEMENT OF HON. RYAN CROCKER, FORMER AMBASSADOR TO IRAQ (2007–2009), DIPLOMAT IN RESIDENCE, WOODROW WILSON SCHOOL, PRINCETON UNIVERSITY

Ambassador CROCKER. Thank you, Madam Chairwoman, Ranking Member Moulton, members of the subcommittee. It is an honor to be here today.

I must say it is a lot more fun being on the outside panel than on the panel that will follow us. I think you both have hit on the essential fact here. The Islamic State is, in essence, not a military problem. Its existence is a symptom of a much deeper problem.

I went through a couple of years in Iraq, 2007 to 2009, the time of the surge. Al Qaeda in Iraq, the forerunner of Islamic State, was a key target of ours and the Iraqis. But even at the height of the surge, we could never absolutely eliminate them. Badly weakened, but still there, parts and pockets of Mosul, and a fluid presence up the Euphrates River Valley.

Why? Because, again, with all that the surge achieved politically, as well as militarily, we saw a period there when the Iraqi Arab Sunnis came back into government, when Prime Minister Maliki took on the Sadrist forces in Basra, throughout the south, and in Baghdad itself, but there still lingered an abiding mistrust on the part of some communities, the Sunni Arabs in particular, of what would happen next.

And that gave Al Qaeda in Iraq space enough to survive. So here we are on the brink of a decisive military difficulty—or victory. But what we have to be able to do is win the peace. Madam Chairwoman, that is not going to happen unless this administration decides that Iraq is a national security priority.

Sadly, if there is a chance to get this right, it will be in Iraq. Syria has, I am afraid, quite a ways to burn before you can talk about an effective political process there. And that is going to take a lot of sustained effort. It will require a Secretary of State who is willing to go to Baghdad, spend time there, get to know the politicians, get a feel for what is possible and what isn't, and in so doing have the full backing of the President.

If we do less than that, I fear that we will see another slide downhill. We can look at Iraq itself or we can look at another example, say, Afghanistan after the defeat of the Soviets. We decided our work then was done. We pulled out. On the way out, we sanctioned Pakistan, who had been our most allied of allies, and that act incidentally reverberates today why the Pakistanis hedge their bets. They think we are going to pull out again. And I do commend the administration for making it quite clear that we are not talking about calendars anymore, but we are talking about conditions.

So it is going to take a formidable political effort to bring things to a better place in Iraq. Madam Chairwoman, we are hardwired into their political system. I found during my time there that we could be the catalyst that made good things happen, but we would have to get something from one party conditionally, take that to the other party, and we found that when we did that some of the time they would give things to us to work that they couldn't do directly with each other.

So, Madam Chairwoman, I understand that people in this country are tired of the never-ending wars in Iraq, now in Syria, that the Hill is tired of this conflict. I get it about being tired. I spent 7 years of my life post-9/11 in Pakistan, Iraq, and Afghanistan. So I know about tired.

But there are worse things. When we decided that we would not intervene or continue our presence in Afghanistan, the totally predictable civil war broke out between rival Afghan factions, culminating in the victory of the Taliban, and that was the road to 9/11. Policies have consequences. The absence of policies have consequences. So again, I commend you, Madam Chairwoman, the ranking member, for bringing us together at this time to concentrate on how we might get it right.

Thank you, Madam Chairwoman.

[The prepared statement of Ambassador Crocker can be found in the Appendix on page 44.]

Mrs. HARTZLER. Thank you, Ambassador.

Dr. Pollack.

STATEMENT OF DR. KENNETH M. POLLACK, RESIDENT SCHOLAR, AMERICAN ENTERPRISE INSTITUTE

Dr. POLLACK. Like my predecessor, Ambassador Crocker, and as you all pointed out in your opening statements, I too am very concerned about the political repercussions of the future of Iraq and American policy there.

I guess I am heartened that we Americans now duly intone that victory in Iraq or any of the Middle East wars will not be won by military forces alone. But I am nevertheless disappointed and frustrated that we rarely ever walk—sorry, walk the walk even though we have learned to talk the talk. The one time when we actually got it right was, of course, when Congressman Moulton and Ambassador Crocker were in Iraq. And I do not see the willingness of the level of preparations on the part of this administration that we saw at that time.

I would like to use my opening statement to just lay the groundwork for what I envision as being necessary for a post-Daesh [ISIS] American commitment to Iraq. And I am going to be very brief to just sketch out the broad framework. But I think it is important to start talking through the details of what is going to be necessary, because again, as Ambassador Crocker knows better than any of us, in Iraq in particular, the devil is in the details. To talk about things just kind of in a broad airy-fairy way and simply say that we need to be there is not going to be helpful.

We need to talk about what it means to be there. We need to talk about what engagement looks like and in particular—and, again, as both you, Madam Chairwoman, and Congressman Moulton, and Ambassador Crocker have all emphasized—we need to be focused on Iraq's politics and how the United States can help move Iraq's politics forward.

Now, all that said, it does start with the military side. Yes, we have won an important victory over Daesh. That is a useful step forward. But we all know that Iraq's security is not going to simply be perfect moving forward. It is going to require residual efforts, and in particular it is going to require a residual American force in the country.

That force's mission will be primarily political. Yes, there are military things that it can and should do, but we need to focus on its political role as being the most important of all, and that—it needs to be able to reassure Iraqis that force will not be used against them, including by their own government or by quasi-governmental entities.

That force needs to be able to prevent the re-politicization of the Iraqi military. And it needs to maintain the combat and logistical capabilities of the Iraqi military that we have so painstakingly built and then abandoned and rebuilt repeatedly but that is critical to allowing the Iraqi government to maintain a monopoly on the use of violence.

All of that is going to require a stay-behind American force, and I would argue that it needs to be bigger rather than smaller to serve these political purposes. If you said to me we would put 25,000 or keep 25,000 troops in Iraq, I would throw a party. I imagine that that might be a bridge too far politically, but I think the 10,000 would be perfectly adequate. But we need to be thinking fairly large for these political reasons.

Shifting quickly over to the political and economic dimensions, which are, as we have all agreed, far more important, we need to recognize that we have a moment now. Iraqis are gleeful that they have defeated ISIS. They are desirous of a better future. They want their government to work better. And they are hopeful that they will get it, but they have been frustrated so many times in the past, we shouldn't assume that they are going to remain patient for all that long. And the problem is, when they grow frustrated, they begin taking unilateral actions that lead them back down the path of civil war.

We need to help the Iraqi government to start to deliver right now, soon, in particular, before their elections. We can't rebuild the country completely. We cannot even help the Iraqis do so. We can't turn it into Switzerland. What we can do is to start programs that are going to give the Iraqis a sense of progress moving forward, a sense that their government can deliver, a sense that the United States is committed to them and their government, and the hope for a better future.

If we can do that—and I have outlined a number of specific projects in my written testimony—if we can do that moving forward, we will keep the Iraqis committed to this political process. That is what we have to have, that is what we need for Iraq to succeed over the long term, that kind of a start. If we don't, we are likely to be repeating our mistakes all over again.

[The prepared statement of Dr. Pollack can be found in the Appendix on page 52.]

Mrs. HARTZLER. Thank you very much. Dr. Lynch.

STATEMENT OF DR. MARC LYNCH, PROFESSOR OF POLITICAL SCIENCE, THE GEORGE WASHINGTON UNIVERSITY

Dr. LYNCH. Thank you, Madam Chairwoman, and Ranking Member Moulton. It is a real honor to be here on a panel with Ambassador Crocker and Ken Pollack. And it is quite an experience to be sitting here in 2017 and largely agree with each other on the major issues, which would not have happened in 2007. And that I think is grounds for hope, that there actually is, I think, a bipartisan sense now of the urgency of having a sustained commitment to getting Iraq right. And I think that is something to build upon.

What is more, as we have heard, I think there is also almost a unanimous consensus among analysts across all stripes that if we hope to actually contain, degrade, and defeat ISIS, we are going to need some kind of sustained political economic reconstruction strategy and the idea of the primacy of the political is something which I think was not present before. And again, this is grounds for hope. I think we agree on the diagnosis in ways which I think was not true before.

So in my written testimony, I offer I think some fairly detailed discussion of a number of issues. I just want to highlight several which I think would be useful for us to think about now and hopefully have time to discuss.

The first is, as Ken said, that there is a window of opportunity now, but it won't last for long. I think that we recently published— in the page I edit for the Washington Post, we published a piece by an Iraqi pollster who found really quite remarkable findings, found 51 percent of Sunnis now saying that the country is going in the right direction, 71 percent of Sunnis saying that they had favorable views of Prime Minister Abadi. In 2014, the same pollster found 5 percent of Sunnis said the same about Prime Minister Maliki.

This is directly and clearly tied to the national campaign to defeat ISIS and liberate those areas. But it also is fleeting, because the conditions under which these people who have been liberated, conditions they are living in are terrible. They are being sustained by a massive international humanitarian effort which has been supported and coordinated extremely well by the coalition, but in a sense it is standing in for the Iraqi state and providing the necessary means of survival for the millions of people who would be liberated from ISIS.

This is a testament to a successful coordination of an unprecedented humanitarian response, but it is also dangerous, because when the next humanitarian crisis emerges and the international NGOs [nongovernmental organizations] move on, who is going to be taking care of all of these people who are not currently being tied to the Iraqi state?

And so one of the most important things I think we need to have on the agenda is a sustained transition strategy moving from disaster relief and crisis relief to a sustainable standard for providing services, goods, and critically, governance for the people in these liberated areas. I know planning of that kind is going on now. It is extremely important that it be fully funded and made equal and parallel to the military track.

I think that we all probably have thoughts on the impact of the Kurdish referendum and the crisis that I think it has sparked. I think at this point all we need to say is that it is urgently necessary that we take whatever effort is needed to calm things down and to try and stop the politicians on all sides, both inside the country and outside the country, from taking escalatory steps. We have to keep the dialogue going. And I think this is pretty important for maintaining the campaign against ISIS.

I think that for all of the military issues, I think that I would come back again and again to the fundamental problem, which is a crisis of state capacity in Iraq. We have consistently seen the inability to construct state institutions which are accountable, effective, authoritative, and honest.

And I think this is at the root of Sunni alienation; this is at the root of the inability of the government of Iraq to provide vital services, electricity, health, everything that you might think of, not necessarily in the capital, but in the rural areas and the Sunni areas, the places where you are likely to see a reimagined ISIS insurgency take root.

And so I think that it is easy to say that we need a whole-of-government approach, we need to have the politics and the economics, along with the military, but I would actually hope that we take seriously as a government the actual primacy of these issues. If we do not find ways to actually have the Iraqi government with our assistance provide sustainable and meaningful quality of life, accountable, transparent, and honest governance to the people across the core constituencies of the regime, then we are going to see almost inevitably major problems to come.

The other point that I would like to make, which I think is the one area where we might have some disagreements on the panel, is that of course what happens in Iraq is unfolding in the midst of ongoing political tension and competition with Iran. And there are major issues in how we should be thinking about our relationship with Iran, the nuclear deal, the spread of Shiite militias. These are important and vital issues.

But I would simply put out there for discussion that Iraq is the single worst place where we could attempt to push back on Iranian influence in the region, and that we should prioritize the stabilization of Iraq and trying to maintain the fragile Iraqi political consensus first, and find other arenas where we might try and push back or contain Iranian influence.

Thank you.

[The prepared statement of Dr. Lynch can be found in the Appendix on page 69.]

Mrs. HARTZLER. Thank you, Dr. Lynch. And you hit on there in your last comment a point that I was going to start off with my questioning, and that was dealing with Iran.

It has been interesting to watch their burgeoning role there in this recent conflict and then taking so much control of various militias and "assisting" quote, unquote. But, Ambassador Crocker, I thought you had some interesting comments in your testimony that says some in the country believe that cooperation with Iran in confronting ISIL is possible and desirable. He said it is neither; Iran does not feel threatened by ISIL.

And then you go on that these units are potentially greater threat to Iraqi stability and our interests than ISIL was. That really—this paragraph jumped out at me. So I would like to hear from you your thoughts on the threat potentially of Iran and the advances that they have made in the country of Iraq and then how you think we ought to deal with that, and then I will probably turn to the other witnesses, too, to kind of get an overview of this situation, because as you said, Dr. Lynch, this is a very important issue we have to deal with.

Ambassador CROCKER. Thank you, Madam Chairwoman. It is indeed a critical issue.

What we find today is that Iranian influence in Iraq is at an all-time high, both directly and indirectly through the so-called Popular Mobilization Units that are far more under the control of Tehran than they are of Baghdad. It is important, I think, to take a step back and ask why. Why are the Iranians doing this?

Biography and history are important. Qasem Soleimani, the leader of Iran's Quds Force, their external operations element, commissioned in the Iranian army a couple of months before Iraq invaded Iran. He served through 8 years of that horrific war. It would be like a British subaltern going through the Western Front not for 4 years, but for 8.

So what do people like Qasem Soleimani think about when they think about Iraq? Never again. Never again will there be an Iraq that could present an existential threat to the Iranian nation. So their interest is not stability in Iraq. It is the opposite, to maintain a maximum level of influence, but also to ensure that the Iraqi government can never quite get its balance. And they are doing a pretty good job of it.

So while I certainly don't urge a military confrontation with Iran in Iraq, I do think we need to be clear-eyed about this. Their objectives in no way harmonize with ours. And we are going to have to figure out how we can ramp up and give the Iraqi government and people some choices over influence that they currently don't have, because with our absence, the Iranian presence is really the only game in town.

Mrs. HARTZLER. Thank you. Dr. Pollack, do you have some thoughts on that?

Dr. POLLACK. Thank you very much, Madam Chairwoman.

I feel like I may be somewhere in between my two panelists both on this issue as well as physically. I start by agreeing with Ambassador Crocker that Iran's interests are ultimately not our interest in Iraq, that Iran's influence there has grown disproportionately, and that ultimately it should be a goal of American policy to limit Iran's influence in Iraq, recognizing that it will never be zero because of their proximity to one another.

That said, I also felt very strongly about some of Marc Lynch's comments. I think that Dr. Lynch is absolutely correct that we are in a precarious moment. And I don't think that Ambassador Crocker was saying otherwise. This is part of the trick moving forward in Iraq, which is right now Iran does have enormous influence in Iraq. Right now, a great many Iraqi politicians are very frightened of the Iranians. And it is going to take them a lot to get them to the point where they trust us enough to simply give the stiff arm to the Iranians.

I also agree that while I am a strong proponent of pushing back on the Iranians across the region—in fact, I am testifying tomorrow before the House Foreign Affairs Committee on exactly that topic—

I agree with the statement that Dr. Lynch made that Iraq is not the place for that, right?

There are a lot of things that we need to do in Iraq. They are important to us on their own terms. Iraq is not the right arena for competition with Iran because of Iran's greater influence there and the fragility of the Iraqi system.

I will simply say that I think that where we ought to focus our efforts, and again I think this is very much consonant both with Ambassador Crocker's remarks and with his own experience, is on building up the Iraqi government and helping the Iraqis to re-achieve their own unity, certainly among Arab, Sunni, and Shia.

You know, the moment where we had the greatest success against Iran in Iraq after the 2003 invasion was in the spring of 2008, when the Iraqi government then led by Prime Minister Nouri al-Maliki, sent mostly Sunni brigades down to Basra to drive the Shia Jaish al-Mahdi, backed by Iran, out of the Shia city of Basra.

And what was so amazing to me—and I was in Basra right after the operation—was how the Shia welcomed these mostly Sunni troops, because they saw them as simply Iraqis who were here to drive out the foreigners, the Persians. If we can get the Iraqis back to that point, where they once again feel like Iraqis and not just Sunni and Shia, they will do a far more effective job than we can in driving the Iranians out.

The trick is exactly as Ambassador Crocker pointed out to be able to do that and to do it at a moment when the Iranians are very influential in Iraq and watching to see what our next move is.

Mrs. HARTZLER. Thank you very much. Dr. Lynch.

Dr. LYNCH. Great, thank you. And I think I am not as far away from Ken on the analysis as I am physically. So that is good.

So I think that you have to begin from the recognition that as Ambassador Crocker said, Iran's role in Iraq is not going to disappear, for reasons of geography, of sectarian affiliation, of deep economic investment, widespread personal relationships, and their cultivation of a portfolio of political allies and proxies not only the Shiite side, but across the entire spectrum. Iran I think has done a very good job of embedding itself deeply in the texture and the fabric of Iraqi politics.

But this is not uncontroversial. And we actually are in a moment where there is increasing sign of resistance within unexpected communities to a dominant Iranian role; not the existence of an Iranian role, but a dominant Iranian role. And here I think is where the place for the United States is less, in my opinion, about pushing back on Iran directly as it is building up the Iraqi state and giving a professional bureaucracy, a professional military, which can become the foundation of the kind of national politics that Dr. Pollack was describing.

And there I think there are real things that we can do which do not have to be cast in a confrontational way and don't, hopefully, have the risk of overturning this extremely delicate political moment. Of course, Ambassador Crocker is right about this, as he is about all things, in terms of the lack of strategic harmony between the United States and Iran in Iraq, but I would say that in the crisis moment of 2014, I think this was less the case.

When it appeared that Baghdad was at the brink of falling and that there was a real perception that the whole thing could come falling apart, there was a convergence on the need to protect the Iraqi state, prevent the advance of ISIS, and work together in a pragmatic way.

And this was something which was never going to last, but if you hadn't seen the Popular Mobilization Units going to the front at the time they did, we could be having a very different conversation right now about a shattered and lost Iraqi state. And that is an important thing to remember.

Not all of the PMF [Popular Mobilization Forces] units are the same. Some of them are I would say functionally the equivalent of the Sahwa, the Awakening Brigades. Some of them are straight-up Iranian proxy forces. And having a differentiated view of that is quite important.

When you have Muqtada al-Sadr going to Saudi Arabia, when you have the appearance of outreach from key Shia constituencies out into the Sunni Arab world, these are important things which I think should be used diplomatically and not dismissed purely on sectarian grounds.

And so I think that what we should be thinking about is creating a place for the United States to be the actor that is supporting governance in Iraq and providing services and supporting a project of state first, politics first, rather than trying to compete with Iran on its own terms in those sorts of ways.

Mrs. HARTZLER. Thank you. I am going to turn to the ranking member now, but I will want to follow up at some point if you don't address it in—the willingness of the Iranians to allow for a consolidated government to form with significant amount of Sunni involvement in that. But we can come back later.

Now turn to Ranking Member Moulton.

Mr. MOULTON. Thank you, Chairwoman Hartzler.

And as someone who witnessed firsthand the influence of Iran in Iraqi politics and, frankly, in military affairs, I just want to emphasize my agreement with the importance of these questions. It is hard, I think, to see how if Iran is fundamentally opposed to our interests in building an Iraqi state, we are going to make this work without confronting that threat, as well. So thank you very much.

Gentlemen, you have I think all agreed, remarkably so, on the importance of the primacy, to use one of your words, of a political effort here and in building the Iraqi state. You have also—Ken, you talked about—Dr. Pollack, you talked about the value of 10,000 troops, maybe even 25,000 troops. We are going to ask the administration from their witnesses how they are prepared to execute such a political plan or if they are prepared to do so at all.

But could you talk for a minute each of you about why this is worth it? Why is it worth the United States investment to put in 10,000 troops if their effort—even if their effort is mainly political? Why is it worth the investment of State Department resources and aid and development resources to build up the Iraqi state?

We have been there a long time. And many Americans are asking, why don't we just pull out and go home? And, Ambassador Crocker, you referred to this a little bit in your introduction, but just explain to the American people why this investment is worthwhile and why now is the right time to make it. Ambassador Crocker, you are welcome to start. Thank you.

Ambassador CROCKER. Thank you, Congressman Moulton. What we are seeing in the region, potentially in Iraq, is not just the overthrow of regimes, but the collapse of states. And sadly, when states collapse, other forces will fill the void, as we have seen. I would call it a failure of governance throughout the region. The modern Middle East is about 100 years old. In that time, that chronic failure of governance has led to crisis after crisis, and I would argue has brought the region to the point it is at today, which is deeply dangerous not only for the region, but for the world, including ourselves.

So there is a fundamental choice here. Either we continue as we have been doing, in which case I think you are going to see Islamic State 2.0, as Islamic State was Al Qaeda in Iraq 2.0. That is not in our interests any more than watching Afghanistan spiral down in the 1990s, again, the rise of the Taliban and the road to 9/11.

Congressman, I have heard much in my career about a failure of intelligence leading to this or that. There is some truth in it. But it is not the whole truth. I call it a failure of imagination that we cannot imagine how bad things can really get. We couldn't imagine that Iranian- and Syrian-backed elements in Lebanon would blow up first the American embassy—I was a survivor of that attack— and later the Marine barracks.

We can't imagine how Iran could move into Iraq through the creation of these proxies. And Dr. Lynch is absolutely right, there is a spectrum here. But the weight on that spectrum is toward the Iranian-influenced units. We——

Mr. MOULTON. Mr. Ambassador, is there anyone in the United States government who imagined how bad Syria would be today?

Ambassador CROCKER. In a word, Congressman, no. And that is what I mean about a failure of imagination. Analysts need to think outside the box. They need to think as though there were no box. I could not have imagined when I left Iraq in the early spring of 2009 that it would descend to the point it is at now. And it is a sharp reminder that you don't end wars by withdrawing your forces. You simply cede the battlespace to others more determined.

Mr. MOULTON. Thank you, Mr. Ambassador. Dr. Pollack.

Dr. POLLACK. Thank you very much, Congressman. I am privileged to get to go around this country and give talks on the Middle East, and I get asked this question frequently. And I will give you the answer more or less that I give them.

The first answer that I give is the relationship to our economy. And I have got to use a four-letter word. It is actually a three-letter word, but it comes out as a four-letter word, and that is oil. We are all infatuated with shale. The truth of the matter is, though, that the world still runs on oil and that Middle East is a major producer of oil, and Iraq currently is the fourth-largest oil producer in the world.

Now, could North American shale make up for the complete loss of Iraqi oil? Maybe. I don't think that anybody really wants to find out. And what we have seen in the past is that oil crises have been major problems for the U.S. economy, causing some of the worst post-war recessions that we have experienced. Until we can do better with weaning ourselves off of oil and finding new sources of it, the Middle East is going to matter and Iraq is going to be critical.

Beyond that is the point that Ambassador Crocker was making. When I go around the country, I typically—you have a line that I have been using for over a decade about how the United States is not like an American city in the southwest. But given the tragic events that have unfolded there in the last couple of days, I am going to refrain from making that comparison and simply say that the problem that we have found with civil wars is that they spread. They don't stay contained.

There is a very extensive body of scholarly work that demonstrates what scholars call the contagion effect, that civil wars in one country destabilize and then cause civil wars in neighboring states. As you pointed out, Syria helped push Iraq back into civil war, and together they have created a mini-civil war in Turkey. In its day, civil war between Israelis and Palestinians caused civil war in Jordan, which then caused civil war in Lebanon, which then caused civil war in Syria.

And as you also alluded to, Ambassador Crocker's point about a failure of imagination, I have got a pretty good imagination. And back in 2012, having studied deeply on the literature of civil wars, I was thinking about what the Syrian civil war could mean for the Middle East and for the world, and I remember as I was writing a piece asking myself, should I point out that if this got really bad, it could start to affect Europe? And I decided I shouldn't, because people would think my imagination was running away with itself.

Well, it not only affected Europe, it helped cause the British to pull out of the EU [European Union], okay? Even I couldn't imagine that. Right? But that is the problem with these kinds of civil wars. They don't stay contained. They spill over. If we simply walk away from Iraq and allow it to descend back into civil war, we don't know what comes next. Kuwait, Jordan, maybe Iran, maybe we would think that was good, at least in the short run. Saudi Arabia. These are countries which at some point we can't possibly accept. They will gut our economy.

Mr. MOULTON. Thank you, Dr. Pollack. Dr. Lynch.

Dr. LYNCH. Thank you. So for the record, I don't agree that we should have 10,000 troops in Iraq or 25,000 troops. I don't think that we have to go to zero, and I think there is a good argument made for the residual—kind of a residual force of trainers and embedded kind of small units.

But I don't think that we should be thinking about it in terms of putting a long-term 10,000, 25,000 permanent U.S. military garrison in Iraq. I think that would actually put us back in an unhealthy place where we were before the withdrawal.

I think what we have now is a situation where we are there at the request of the Iraqi government. There is actually political support at a fairly wide level for the American presence there. And we have a bipartisan support for what we have in Iraq now. So the politics are in some ways right for a small residual force for the United States in both the United States and in Iraq.

But moving to have this kind of long-term, large-scale U.S. military presence I think risks unsettling both of those consensuses that have become a flashpoint for political controversy here in the

United States and would draw a great deal of unwanted attention inside of Iraq to this renewed notion of a permanent American military presence. I actually think that is not a good idea, but we can continue to discuss that.

On the question of why it is worth it, I want to also perhaps be a little contrary here, as well, to break the comity that we have had to this point. I think that this is ultimately up to the Iraqis to choose. This is not an American decision. If the Iraqis choose to create a sectarian and exclusionary state, to not confront corruption, to allow the rural and Sunni areas to go without governance and to not try and meet the needs of their Sunni population, then nothing we do can help them. We could have 10,000 troops, we could have 50,000 troops. We could do almost anything and it won't help.

The choice is up to them. And the hope that we have is that after having faced the crisis of 2014, they are now willing and able to make those choices, to create the kind of functional state which can partner with the United States on equal terms. And I think that is the direction we need to be moving in, is having a partnership which is based upon not just keeping a presence in Iraq no matter what, but to have it based on the notion that this is the type of state that we want to support and giving the types of assistance that can actually support that kind of state. Different way of thinking about it, but I think an important difference.

Mr. MOULTON. Dr. Lynch, I think I understand your position. Do you agree that we have a national security interest in the Middle East and in Iraq?

Dr. LYNCH. Oh, absolutely. And I agree 100 percent with—

Mr. MOULTON. But do you think ultimately we should let the Iraqis decide on whether we pursue that national security interest?

Dr. LYNCH. No. My point is that if the Iraqis make the wrong choices in terms of the type of state they build, then we can waste an enormous amount of American blood and treasure accomplishing very little, because ultimately if they recreate the sectarianism, corruption, and state failure which led to 2014, then we cannot achieve our national security goals as I think we all agree that they should be defined.

Mr. MOULTON. Do you think we can have any influence on that decision?

Dr. LYNCH. We can have influence on it. And that I think is what I was trying to say about the political underpinnings that now exist for a sustained partnership between this Iraqi government and the United States. And otherwise I wouldn't be recommending that we have this kind of long-term commitment and focusing on building the economic, political, and military degrees of cooperation. I absolutely think that this is a moment where we do have that kind of influence and we certainly have the interest to sustain it.

But I want to warn against unconditional commitment even if you don't have the foundations that would make it possible. That is what I am most worried about, is that by giving a blank check, we could enable exactly the kinds of dysfunction that created 2014 in the first place.

Mr. MOULTON. Thank you. And if I may just conclude with one very brief question, if you could answer in one sentence or less, just each of you, you have agreed so much on the need for the primacy of a political commitment and how that must lead our efforts in all that we do.

I was a frequent critic of the Obama administration because I didn't feel that they understood this. And they responded to the ISIS crisis by just sending military trainers in, which didn't really do much to fix Iraqi politics. We got lucky with the new prime minister, but I don't think that we can claim much credit for the political improvement that has happened there.

Do you think this administration understands this and is prepared to make a political commitment the prime commitment? Ambassador Crocker.

Ambassador CROCKER. Yes. I do think that is the case. When you look at leaders like Secretary Mattis, he certainly knows Iraq up close and personal. The national security adviser, H.R. McMaster, the same, both Iraq and Afghanistan.

Mr. MOULTON. Dr. Pollack, do you agree?

Dr. POLLACK. I will perhaps refine Ryan's answer slightly and say I think that there are those in this administration who absolutely understand it and are absolutely committed, but they don't seem to yet have a decision made about what their policy is going to be.

Mr. MOULTON. Dr. Lynch.

Dr. LYNCH. I have no idea.

Mr. MOULTON. Thank you, Madam Chairwoman.

Mrs. HARTZLER. Thank you. Representative Scott of Georgia.

Mr. SCOTT. Thank you, Madam Chair. Gentlemen, thank you for being here.

As we talk about securing the peace, it seems to me that the more pressure we put on these groups in one area, they simply move to other areas of ungoverned territory, and there is certainly a tremendous number of areas where they can go in northeast Africa, the Middle East, where they can—it seems remobilize, re-equip, and come back with maybe a different goal and different strategy.

So my question revolves around that challenge. As we—what would you suggest the best path is to stop what I would call the remobilization or the relocation of the terrorist organizations, where they are able to regroup and come back and attack in another country?

Ambassador CROCKER. It is an important question, Congressman. In one sense, if we can keep them moving around, that keeps them off-balance, but we would have to, again, have the resolve, if they are relocating somewhere else where there is no effective state, pursue them there, not by sending in the 101st, but there are other platforms. You know, the more we can keep them on the defensive, the less likely they are to have the time and the space to plan another major attack into Europe or, God forbid, into this country.

So, again, I would like to say that we could find a way to eliminate this scourge. I don't think that is going to happen anytime soon, but we sure as heck can keep them off-balance, we can trip them so that they have no safe place ultimately in which they can plan strategic-level attacks.

Dr. LYNCH. I think, Representative Scott, that is a great question. And I think it gets to the heart of having to place Iraq within a full-scale regional and international strategy. And so what my comments about trying to build the capacity of the Iraqi state should be read as part of a much wider strategy of trying to rebuild states across the region, and that includes not just rebuilding militaries and counterterrorism units, but actually building governance and actually building accountable states which are responsive to their people that can provide and deliver services.

And so I think that I would absolutely think that you are putting your finger right on the problem with a shattered Middle East, not just a shattered Iraq. That said, I think Iraq is actually a distinctively important place for both Al Qaeda and for ISIS. This is where Al Qaeda transformed for the first time into a serious insurgency back with Zarqawi. This is where the remnants of that insurgency became the Islamic State and were able to move into Syria and take over these parts of Iraq.

I think that a defeat and removal or at least a strategic defeat of the Islamic State in Iraq will have much greater impact on its appeal and attractiveness and power across the rest of the world than pretty much any other place.

Dr. POLLACK. Congressman Scott, I will simply add, first, I agree very much with the points that Dr. Lynch made. I think he has got it spot on. I will start by saying that we need to separate out two different problems, the problems of the civil wars in Iraq, Syria for that matter, and the problem of transnational terrorism. They are ultimately related but distinct topics.

And I will start by saying the line—to use a line from a friend of mine within the Trump administration, it is not the case that Iraq and Syria are in civil war because ISIS is there. ISIS is there because Iraq and Syria are in civil war.

Mr. SCOTT. That is right.

Dr. POLLACK. And so point number one is, we do need to stabilize these different countries. At the end of the day, though, you are absolutely right, Congressman, there will always be ungoverned spaces on the map. And the terrorist groups will always seek refuge there.

The hope has to be that if we can deny them recruits, because there aren't large numbers of people in places like the Middle East who are desperately unhappy and looking to kill someone as a result of that, you can cut off the flow of oxygen, you can diminish their strength, and then both defensive measures, like those that we put in place after 9/11, and offensive measures, such as special forces operations, drone strikes, et cetera, can diminish the threat to the point where it isn't significant at all.

Mr. SCOTT. Madam Chair, I am almost out of time. One of the other things I think that we need to talk through is whether or not when we have small pockets where we have 10 or 15 or 20 that we believe to be or know to be through intelligence part of one of the terrorist organizations, that we should go ahead and take them out prior to them recruiting and becoming a significantly larger and more capable group. It seems to me that we would do better to—if we know they are what they are, we are not going to fix that, so we might as well help the rest of the world. Thank you.

Mrs. HARTZLER. Thank you. Mr. O'Halleran.

Mr. O'HALLERAN. Thank you, Madam Chair.

Dr. Pollack, you stated about the stay behind and an indeterminate amount of time. This is the second time today we have heard the issue of our troops staying behind. Afghanistan was the other issue earlier today.

And I don't know what is going to happen in western Syria especially, but if we have potential there, then we have the Kurdish Iraqi situation, and are we going to be peacekeepers along that? Or how are we going to get the U.N. involved?

So what does stay behind mean? And what is the implications of that on the geopolitical issues within that area?

Dr. POLLACK. Thanks very much, Congressman. And I think this is an important set of questions for this committee in particular to dig into.

As I noted earlier, Iraq is a quintessential civil war. We know a lot about these civil wars. We know a lot about how to bring them to peaceful ends and prevent them from recurring. What the history of these civil wars have demonstrated over and over and over again is that you need to have three conditions in place. One, what is called a hurting stalemate, where none of the groups believes that they can win a military victory, and in fact they have real incentives to stop fighting.

Second, there needs to be a political power-sharing arrangement. And third, there needs to be some institution that remains in place for a period of time, typically 10 to 20 years, that guarantees or at least reassures people that conditions one and two will continue to obtain. Historically, the best institution for that is an external peacekeeping force.

And I would argue that that is, at least in Iraq—I am not an Afghan expert, I am not going to speak to Afghanistan—that is a different mission. It is a war in a very different state of affairs. But in Iraq, that is how we should be thinking about the U.S. force there, as a peacekeeping force.

What we have seen is, peacekeeping forces need to start with a certain size to establish presence. And my point about the numbers is driven by State Department—sorry, by CENTCOM [U.S. Central Command] and DOD [Department of Defense] planning for the stay behind force. In 2009, 2010, 2011, the actual military force in Iraq led by General Lloyd Austin formulated a plan. They believed that the right number was somewhere between 22,000 and 25,000 troops to maintain that presence. The Department of Defense refined that and said we think we can do it with 10,000 troops.

I think that those numbers are more or less correct, given where Iraq is today. Now, over time, I suspect that those numbers can come down, because what you see in these civil wars is that over time the communities rebuild their trust and that presence can become increasingly symbolic. So this is not Korea. We are not going to need a large force there ready to fight a major war at a moment's notice.

But what we do need to be thinking about is the political role of these troops in reassuring Iraqis that they are not going to have violence used against them, that their military is not going to be re-politicized, and their military isn't going to lose the capability to put down bad actors when it is necessary to do so.

And as I said, I think that the numbers formulated first by USF–I [U.S. Forces–Iraq], General Austin and his men, and then refined by the Department of Defense, are exactly where we ought to be thinking. Those were the right numbers at exactly the same moment in time.

Mr. O'HALLERAN. Thank you, Doctor.

Ambassador Crocker, Mr. Scott brought up the issue concerning other locations in the world about terrorism. And we have a significant amount of—a lot of this is going to be requiring State Department work. The military can't do everything, and we would rather have no war than a war.

So do you feel that the current proposed cuts to the State Department, given North Korea and all the other issues going on around this world, are a position that we should be taking?

Ambassador CROCKER. Thank you for asking that, Congressman. In a word, no. What we are seeing, frankly, is not simply a budget cut in megatons. We were seeing, I think, an effort to deconstruct the State Department and the Foreign Service.

And I can tell you, if that is not reversed, this is something we are going to be paying for, for a very long time. If we have to cut back our intake, then you are going to have that gap moving forward for the next 20 years, where you don't have the senior officer cadre who are fluent in foreign languages, who know these countries and cultures, who know how to deal with it.

So I can't put it strongly enough. This is a very, very serious issue. If we don't want to have to fight a whole lot more wars, then you need a strong, well-resourced Foreign Service to go out there and do what may be possible to see that the troops don't have to come in.

Mr. O'HALLERAN. Thank you, Madam Chair. I yield.

Mrs. HARTZLER. Thank you. Representative Cheney.

Ms. CHENEY. Thank you, Madam Chairwoman. And thanks very much to all of the witnesses here today.

Ambassador Crocker and I had the privilege of serving together in the State Department. And, Ambassador, you know that I think you are one of the wisest, most thoughtful members of the Foreign Service we have. And I am very grateful for your appearance here today and for your testimony.

Could you talk a little bit about the connection and the relationship between our ability as a nation to influence political events in a place like Iraq and our troops? And in particular, I am thinking about as we surged in 2007, what that meant in terms of our leverage in the country, and how you try to replicate that same kind of political leverage in an environment in which we are not going to have that number of troops on the ground, certainly.

But how do you make sure that the United States, in addition to the—reversing the kinds of cuts that you have talked about, but having the political leverage, is it possible to have the kind of political leverage with all the sides that would be necessary for a political solution in the absence of the kind of military presence that we saw at the moment when our leverage was highest?

Ambassador CROCKER. Thank you, Congresswoman. And I must say, it is very nice to see you sitting there.

We will not have that level of leverage again. But I think we may not need that level. The Iraqi forces after their horrific collapse in 2014 have pulled themselves back together. It is true that the Counter Terrorism Service is carrying out a major part of this. But, you know, there has been progress over these last 2 or 3 years with the Iraqi army generally. So we want to be in a position to continue to encourage that.

We are the United States of America. We do have leverage, should we choose to use it. But that is why, again, I would not make any suggestions on troop levels at this point. We need to see a President engage. We are a Presidential system. If the President isn't decided on what he wants to do, then you start to lose that kind of influence.

So, again, I would like to see the President ask his Secretary of State to go out to Iraq, spend more than 12 hours there, start a process of engagement with not just the current government, but political leaders across the board, and then report back on what is possible and what isn't possible, and to go from there.

Ms. CHENEY. Thank you. And, Dr. Pollack, I walked in as you were saying that there will always be ungoverned areas. And in keeping with the great tradition up here in the House of Representatives, I am not going to let the fact that I walked in two-thirds of the way through stop me from asking you a question.

Talk about the extent to which—you are not saying that we shouldn't be denying safe haven, are you?

Dr. POLLACK. No.

Ms. CHENEY. And so when you—what is that balance? In terms of—we have got to deny safe haven. We have also got to deny recruits. But how can you ensure that we are going to deny safe haven in the absence of, you know, some basic level of troops, American troops on the ground?

Dr. POLLACK. Thank you very much, Congresswoman. It obviously depends on what we are talking about. In places like Iraq, where I think the United States has a clear national interest that goes beyond the mere terrorism problem, I think the presence of troops is warranted, at least for a certain period of time and probably longer than Dr. Lynch believes is necessary.

There are going to be places, though, like Mali, where I don't think that we are necessarily warranted American military presence because our interests are much narrower, no offense to any Malians who are here or may be thinking about this. But it simply does not rise to the same level as Iraq.

Under those circumstances, I think the United States does need to use other tools available to it, whether it be diplomacy or assistance to the host nation, to try to make these places as unhospitable as possible. I want to agree with Dr. Lynch that the best way to do it is to help these countries repair themselves, an effort that you were trying to lead at least for the Middle East when you were at the State Department. You know better than I do that if you have functional societies——

Ms. CHENEY. You don't cost us votes in here today.

Dr. POLLACK. If you have functioning societies, you are going to have far fewer terrorists.

Ms. CHENEY. Thank you very much. I appreciate it. And I yield back, Madam Chairwoman.

Mrs. HARTZLER. Thank you very much.

Representative Panetta.

Mr. PANETTA. Thank you, Madam Chairman. Gentlemen, thank you for your time, your preparation, and your testimony today. I apologize for being late.

In regards to that sort of infrastructure development, I guess I saw something—or the RAND Corporation did something about Mosul's infrastructure, when—its water, its sanitation, its power capacity is not doing that well. What are the current efforts right now, be it through the United States government or be it through the Iraqi government, anything at all to help develop that? Because clearly that will play a part in its self-governing.

Dr. LYNCH. There have been pretty massive efforts to deal with the humanitarian crisis dimension of it. There is over 150 NGOs on the ground working, coordinated by the coalition, and there has been a really quite remarkable effort at the humanitarian relief side. But the reconstruction side is still a blank slate. And I think that in the midst of crisis, it is very difficult to plan for the long term and to begin reconstruction when the fighting is still going on, which I think is why having this hearing right now is so important, because now is the time to get those plans into place, make sure they are fully resourced and coordinated.

One of the other problems is that is going to have to be linked up to the political development inside of Iraq. In other words, there has to be some sense of what governance is going to look like in Mosul, who is going to be responsible for the administration of these reconstruction projects, who will get political credit for them, and how will they be linked into the broader Iraqi political system. To me, this is the absolute most important thing for us to be looking at right now.

Mr. PANETTA. Okay.

Ambassador CROCKER. Well, thank you, Congressman. It is an important question, obviously.

One of the problems the Iraqis confront, and their friends with them, is a diminution of resources. There just isn't that kind of money floating around anymore. They are running a horrific deficit, and you see the consequences.

During my time there in 2007, a decade ago, the prime minister, Nouri al-Maliki, extended the first supplemental budget increase—we taught them a lot of bad habits, and supplemental budgets, of course, would be among them. The prime minister allocated $250 million to the province of Anbar, because he was finally persuaded that if you really want to turn the tide out there against Al Qaeda, support the Awakening. And it worked.

Well, Prime Minister Abadi doesn't really have $250 million to push up to Mosul. So I think the emphasis is going to have to be on, you know, a hard-eyed analysis of what really needs to be done and done quickly to provide momentum for political solutions, but at the same time to be pressing on the issue of governance, because I think we have all said this in one way or the other.

Again, if you want to look through the 100-year history of the modern Middle East, there is one single word that I use, governance, the failure thereof. And that goes back to colonialism and im-perialism, the French and the British, and it runs right up to today. Now we have Islamism, also a failure to govern.

So if you—even if you do have the money for resources, you have got to get the governance thing down and down right, and it is enormously difficult and it is going to take a lot of time. I just hope we are prepared to make that commitment.

Dr. POLLACK. Congressman, if I could just add one point, which is this stuff is very hard to do in the moment, right? We are once again trying to build an airplane in mid-flight, something that we have repeatedly tried to do in Iraq. I would actually argue the time to have dealt with the governance issue in Mosul—in fact, I was arguing it then—was 18 to 24 months ago, when it would have been far easier to deal with. Unfortunately, we didn't, and it is get-ting harder and harder.

We are coming up on elections in Iraq. Inshallah, there will be elections at some point in the spring. The closer we get to those elections, the harder it is going to be for us to deal with many of Iraq's political problems. And as again, Ambassador Crocker knows better than anyone, after those elections, we could face a long and painful process of governance formation. It is why doing this now is so critical and why it is so wonderful that you are taking up this issue now and hopefully can push the administration to engage with it more fully.

Mr. PANETTA. Understood. Thank you. I yield back. Thank you, Madam Chair.

Mrs. HARTZLER. Sure, thank you. And we have more questions, but I know, Dr. Lynch, you have indicated you had a hard stop at 4:30, so if you need to leave, we certainly want to give you the grace to do that. And thank you for coming. Appreciate it.

Dr. LYNCH. Thank you, Chairman. I think my students will un-derstand if I stay for the last few minutes.

Mrs. HARTZLER. Okay, very good. Well, thank you. Representa-tive Suozzi.

Mr. SUOZZI. Thank you, Madam Chairwoman, and thank you to the witnesses again. And I apologize, like the previous few Con-gress Members, for being late here today and for missing so much. And I apologize if I am repeating some things that you have asked earlier.

I am concerned about two complicating factors for the long term in the area. One is the close relationship between Iran and Iraq based upon the fact that major Shia religious sites are located within Iraq. And it is normal for tourists from Iran to come into Iraq on a regular basis. And there is a lot of cultural friendships and relationships based upon these religious sites that have been established over centuries, and how complicating is that factor?

The second factor has been the genocide of Christians and Yazidis and other minority groups within Iraq and Syria. And I just want to get a quick insight from each of you about how compli-cating a factor that will be, those two factors will be going forward.

Ambassador CROCKER. On the first, Congressman, I would cer-tainly never recommend that Iraq take steps to bar Iranian pil-grims from the holy sites in Iraq. You are quite right, those are major pilgrimage destinations, just as we see Muslims from around the world flock to Mecca in Saudi Arabia.

My colleagues have said quite rightly Iran will certainly have influence in Iraq. It is natural, one neighbor to another. But we also need to keep in mind that an agreement on—that they are all Shia together is significant, but there are many, many differences, linguistic, Arabs versus Persians, lots of constraining elements at work, too. So in countering Iranian influence in Iraq, I would go nowhere near an effort to block Iranian pilgrims.

On the plight of the Christians in Iraq and, indeed, in Syria, no question about it. We are reaching the point where we may see the critical weight of the Christian communities, particularly in Iraq, get below the level necessary to sustain their presence. And I would think that that would need to be a very important issue for the administration to take up. But it has to be done delicately. We cannot create a public impression that we are there to defend the Christians. That is sadly only likely to increase the pressures on them.

So this is all tough. It is all complicated. As Dr. Pollack says, you can't do it in the moment. You have got to make the commitment to a long-term, high-level sustained political effort in Iraq and elsewhere in the region.

Mr. SUOZZI. And how do you militate against the influence of the Popular Mobilization Units? I mean, that is—those are all Iranian-backed, right, for the most part?

Ambassador CROCKER. No, sir. I think as Dr. Lynch and Dr. Pollack have both said, they run a spectrum.

Mr. SUOZZI. Okay, you don't have to answer that, then. Anything you want to add, Mr. Pollack?

Dr. POLLACK. I think they are both excellent points, Congressman. And I will simply make some broader points. First, as you point out, as we have talked about repeatedly this afternoon, there are deep interlinkages between Iran and Iraq. And there is nothing that we are going to do that are going to end those.

Likewise, the problems of genocide and intercommunal violence in Iraq are also pervasive. And it is important to remember the words of a very wise man who used to repeatedly say that Iraq is very, very, very, very, very hard and it is very, very, very, very hard all the time. Did I get all the verys?

That said, we also—you know, one of the most remarkable things about Iraq is the ability of this country to overcome all of those problems and all of those interlinkages. We need to remember that in 2007, 2008, when the United States started to reverse the perverse incentives that we created in 2003, 2004, it was incredible how fast Iraq started to turn around.

Now, Iraq was never Switzerland, right? Iraq was not exactly, you know, ready for EU membership. But the change, the direction, the delta was remarkable, and it was incredible to see Iraqis coming together out of a recognition that hanging together was much better than hanging apart.

So it is simply a way of saying that you are right, there are problems, there are complications, we need to be aware of them. That is exactly why we need to plan ahead, why we need to make a big effort, work with the Iraqis, but we also shouldn't just throw up our hands and say this is impossible.

Dr. LYNCH. If I may, the problem of the minorities in Iraq has been an enormous since 2003. You have seen the devastation of minority communities across Iraq, not just Yazidis and the Christians, but beyond. The best protection for minorities is to have a strong and capable Iraqi state that can protect all of its citizens. Trying to single out particular communities for protection I think is very difficult to do, and it is not sustainable in the long term, but making that part of a broader package of building state capacity I think is absolutely vital.

Mr. SUOZZI. I have exceeded my time. Thank you very much, Madam Chairwoman.

Mrs. HARTZLER. You bet. Thank you to each and every one of you. We very much appreciate this. We have more questions we could ask, but we are going to have votes in about a half an hour. We want to get to our second panel. But thank you so much for all your insights and all of your devotion to our country and helping out today.

So let's go ahead and I would like to invite the second panel to the witness table. So we will invite them in.

So as they get settled, I will make some brief introductions. We want to welcome this Department of Defense panel. We have Mr. Mark Swayne, Acting Deputy Assistant Secretary of Defense for Stability and Humanitarian Affairs in the Office of the Assistant Secretary of Defense for Special Operations and Low-Intensity Conflict.

We have Brigadier General James Bierman, director of the Middle East division on the Joint Staff J–5.

We have Mr. Joseph Pennington, Deputy Assistant Secretary for Iraq in the Bureau of Near Eastern Affairs at the Department of State.

And we have Ms. Pamela Quanrud, Director of the Global Coalition to Defeat ISIS at the Department of State.

Due to the time that we have, I think we will forego the opening statements, if we could, since we only have a half an hour before votes. And we want to get right to your thoughts and your insights on things. So thank you so much for being here.

Mr. Pennington, I think I would like to start with you. What can you tell us about conversations between the United States and the government of Iraq? How long do you anticipate having a large military footprint in Iraq? And what is the prospect of executing an agreeable status of forces agreement with Iraq?

Mr. PENNINGTON. Thank you, Madam Chairwoman, and thank you for the opportunity to be here today to testify.

I think I will—on the first part of your question, I will kick a large chunk of that to my DOD colleagues, but I will just comment that I think the success that we—and when I say we, I mean the coalition supporting Iraqi partners on the ground—have had in the fight against ISIS has convinced Iraqi leaders or Iraqi partners, including Prime Minister Abadi, of the efficacy of partnership with U.S. and coalition forces.

The prime minister is open to and enthusiastic about the prospect of continuing that partnership going forward to meet new challenges in Iraq, once the active military operations against ISIS wind down.

Again, I want to not get into too much of the DOD territory here, but I think there is a very good prospect for continuing a security partnership under the strategic framework agreement that we have in place with Iraq. And I think there is a good appetite for that on both sides.

With regard to the part of the question about status of forces, as you may know, we have an exchange of notes that regulates military presence in Iraq now. We believe—and I think my colleagues would say the same—that that is sufficient for our presence as it currently stands, given the purpose and the scope of that relationship.

Maybe I will stop there and invite other comments.

Mrs. HARTZLER. Sure, appreciate your perspective from the Department of State. Department of Defense want to weigh in on that?

Mr. SWAYNE. Thank you, Madam Chairwoman and Ranking Member Moulton and all subcommittee members for having us today. For the issue of the SOFA [Status of Forces Agreement], I agree completely with my State colleague. U.S. forces in Iraq are operating under the 2014 exchange of notes with the government of Iraq. This exchange of notes provides U.S. forces with the appropriate protections and not further commitments—no further commitments are required, so we feel that that exchange of notes is appropriate for right now. Thank you.

Mrs. HARTZLER. Yes, very good. Well, thank you. Mr. Swayne, given continued budget pressures, readiness crises across the military and competing national security interests, how do you expect to achieve our objectives in Iraq?

Mr. SWAYNE. Thank you very much. As we—the DOD mission in Iraq is focused on dealing with ISIS and to deliver them a lasting defeat. I think that is a critical issue for the United States Department of Defense. It is clear that our objective is to defeat ISIS wherever it exists, and in Iraq is a very critical portion of where ISIS remains. Once they are defeated, we think that that defeat will not occur immediately after ISIS loses its territorial control.

ISIS is likely to continue to plot or inspire external attacks, and to deal with that threat, the United States Department of Defense is going to have to have a relationship with the government of Iraq and the Iraqi security forces to require continued training and to effectively secure liberated areas.

Now, the last 3 years of fighting have effectively secured liberated areas, and we have focused on conventional operations. And a new ISIS threat will require proficiency in wide areas of security operations in counterinsurgency, and that is an area I think that we can work with the Iraqi government and the Iraqi military to determine what the needs are going forward with the Iraqi security forces, and that includes the United States and also our coalition partners as we look for the advise-and-assist teams and to work for the future training missions.

Mrs. HARTZLER. But the question was dealing with our budget situation that we have and the readiness crises that we have encountered. So do you have what you need in order to be able to finish the mission there and carry it out? What are areas of concerns that you have or needs that you may have?

Mr. SWAYNE. Yes, ma'am, thank you. With the actual budget numbers and the actual numbers of our troops going forward, that is something that in this unclassified open hearing, we are not prepared to discuss the particulars. It is ongoing right now for the planning within the Department of Defense and to look at what the requirements are with our Iraqi partners and then come back and work with the committee to determine, once we have that plan, in a classified, closed session, then I think we will be ready for an open discussion after that.

But at this time, the details on the budget or the numbers are certainly things that we are concerned about, thinking about. It is very clear to us that in the defeat of ISIS, the long-term defeat of ISIS and a lasting defeat of ISIS, we need to have a strong Iraqi government and a strong Iraqi security forces. And that is certainly at the top of our priority list within the Department. Thank you.

Mrs. HARTZLER. Okay, thank you. Ranking Member Moulton.

Mr. MOULTON. Madam Chairwoman, thank you very much.

Thank you all for joining us here today. As an Iraq war veteran myself, I know that I am joined by several others both in the room, and, General, thank you for your service on the panel. We were in Hillah about the same time in 2003.

I can't tell you how painful it is as an Iraq war veteran now sitting on this committee to see us fighting and refighting so many of the same battles that we fought, that our friends gave their lives for. And so the question that we must ask is, how will this time be different? How do we know that now that ISIS is about defeated there won't be an ISIS 2.0, just as ISIS in many ways is Al Qaeda in Iraq 2.0?

We heard from the expert panel that preceded you how important it is that Iraqi politics be the primary effort. The primacy of the political effort is the phrase that several of the panelists used. But I am not hearing that from you yet. I am hearing about how we are going to ensure we clean up the rest of ISIS and we train the Iraqi military. I haven't heard anything about how we are going to ensure the success of Iraqi politics, which ultimately will prevent us from having to come back and clean up the mess when Iraqi politics fails.

Just before this hearing, I discussed this with Secretary Mattis and General Dunford. And the Chairman and the Secretary agreed that we have to have a political plan. So where is that political plan? How will it be better and different than the political effort in the past to ensure that we don't repeat the same mistakes and find us coming back to Iraq to refight these same battles yet again?

Mr. PENNINGTON. Thank you very much for the question, Congressman. Maybe I will start on that. And I think just as we have approached the military issue—the military side of the relationship with Iraq in this fight against ISIS in a somewhat different way, what we will call by, with, and through, supporting, but having Iraqi partners lead on the ground, building that partnership from the ground up, we believe that the same kind of approach on the political side is the right strategy going forward.

And so we have focused our efforts, our immediate efforts on strengthening Iraq's ability to govern the liberated spaces, and by that I am referring to our efforts towards stabilization.

Mr. MOULTON. Can you just give us an idea of what those efforts are?

Mr. PENNINGTON. Sure. So by stabilization, it is a fairly broad concept, but the way I would define it is to create the conditions on the ground to enable those who have been displaced by the fighting and by the ISIS terrorism to make the decision to return to their homes and live in security, reestablishing their communities, with the support of the Iraqi government.

Behind that Iraqi government support is the United States and our coalition partners. And so we, on the one hand, have spent more than $1.7 billion to deal with the immediate emergency of humanitarian displacement, making sure people can survive when they are displaced, and beyond that and more recently, have worked with our coalition partners through the U.N. Development Program, something called the Funding Facility for Stabilization, to help the Iraqis to go into liberated areas, to rebuild the infrastructure, basic services, water, electricity, schools, health clinics, clearing rubble from the streets, getting some cash into the economy.

Mr. MOULTON. So with all due respect, if we had been here in 2004 or 2005 or 2007 or 2008, it would have been the same thing. How is this time different?

Mr. PENNINGTON. Well, I would suggest, Congressman, that it is a matter of reestablishing government authority in areas where they have been absent, through our consistent support to help strengthen governing institutions, to partner with Iraqis, and we have an excellent partner.

Mr. MOULTON. Sir, I was there last in 2008. We did exactly the same things. How is this time different? How will we ensure that when we do all those same things as we did as the previous panelists mentioned actually quite successfully in 2007, 2008, with over 100,000 troops to assist in the effort, how is this time going to be more successful so it doesn't fall apart again?

Mr. PENNINGTON. On the political side, Congressman, as you know, we are approaching an election season in Iraq. That is something that is going to be—the politics of this are going to be fought out by Iraqis. We have, of course, contacts across a broad range of Iraqis, Sunni, Shia, Kurd minorities.

We are encouraging full participation of all segments. We believe we have the—and there is some polling data to bear this out—that Iraqis are increasingly seeing their governing challenges as requiring national solutions, and so there is a greater sense of an Iraqi national identity, a greater cross-fertilization across sectarian lines.

We would expect in this election to see alliances and coalitions built across sectarian lines which would build a more inclusive governing structure.

Mr. MOULTON. So I appreciate the hopeful description of Iraqi politics. You still haven't said a single thing that we are doing differently. What is the United States doing differently? General, would you care to comment on this, please?

General BIERMAN. I will make a couple comments. And thanks for the question. Based off of the events in 2014, the Iraqi government invited us in. And what occurred with the rapid spread of ISIS was a representation to Iraqis across the spectrum of how bad things could be.

And we have established a trust relationship, military-to-military, but we would be the first ones to tell you that the ultimate success and future of Iraq is political, is economic, and is diplomatic.

Some of the things that I would tell you that I see is different, like you, having made several trips back and forth, I think we have a fragile but responsible Iraqi government. And I think they want a long-term relationship with us, and they have voiced across the military and civilian governance that they want us to stay, because the events of the last 2 years have showed them that they need us.

The other thing I would say is the Iraqis, contrary to some of the experiences you and I have had in the past, not to take anything away from the great efforts of the U.S. military to enable the Iraqi operations, they are fighting their own battles. Over the last year, the Iraqis have suffered tens of thousands of casualties in the fights to liberate their countries.

And I take nothing away from those extraordinary U.S. and coalition service men who have been killed or wounded. God rest their souls. But the Iraqis are carrying this fight on their backs. We are going to have significant challenges as we near the end, as we approach the end of physical ISIS. That has been a unifying factor that has united a lot of disparate elements across the spectrum in Iraq. And we are going to have to work very, very hard politically, diplomatically to knit this fragile Iraqi ecosystem together.

One of the key components of strong governments is going to be efficient and professional Iraqi security forces. So while we stay, you know, focused within our military lane, we very much see that as a means to an end that one of the key factors in enabling the Iraqi government is what we are doing on the military side. Thank you.

Mr. MOULTON. And, General, I agree with everything you said. And that was my experience on the ground in Iraq, too, is I understood how important it was for the politics to follow through. But back in 2008, I felt like we had a lot of political resources in country. As I have been to visit Iraq more recently as a member of this committee, I have repeatedly heard from our State Department and officials on the ground that—and our military—that they don't have the political resources necessary.

Chairman Dunford just a couple of hours ago said—talking about Afghanistan—that we need to push State Department resources further down into the Afghan political system, but we are not doing that yet. Again, has anything changed? Are we doing it now in Iraq where we weren't doing it 6 months or a year ago, so that ultimately where we have not been able to ensure the political success of Iraq in the past, you can now tell me that you have the confidence that we will?

General BIERMAN. I would just simply agree with what you just heard from the Chairman of the Joint Chiefs of Staff, that we would certainly advocate an increased and stronger role from——

Mr. MOULTON. Thank you, General, for your candor.

General BIERMAN [continuing]. From the Department of State. And I think that the folks that they have on the ground are doing remarkable things, but we would support increased efforts in that area.

Mr. MOULTON. Would anyone else on the panel care to comment?

Mr. PENNINGTON. If I might, Congressman, just following up on the general's comments, I think in terms of what is different now, I think one thing that is different is that the Iraqis have seen the terrible cost of political failure up close and the destruction of communities, the destruction, the genocide that has been carried out against various groups by ISIS, and ultimately the destruction of largely Sunni cities, I think has been a very sobering experience for Iraqis across the political spectrum and across sectarian divides.

And I think that is what is driving what I referred to as a more hopeful political picture. There are no political guarantees. And this will be a process that is Iraqi-driven. And we will support in every way that we can, but I think that level of destruction and the level of terror that the population has endured has changed attitudes in Iraq.

Mr. MOULTON. Thank you. Director Quanrud, do you have anything to add?

Ms. QUANRUD. No.

Mr. MOULTON. Mr. Swayne, if I may just briefly ask, do you agree with the consensus of the expert panel that the primary effort must be political in Iraq at this stage?

Mr. SWAYNE. Yes, absolutely. I think there is no doubt about, for sustainable security, for sustainable stability in Iraq over the next few months, years, we have to have a clear—so I agree with that wholeheartedly and to respond a little bit to the question before, DOD, it is our whole-of-government approach working by, with, and through. We certainly have to work very closely—we, the Department of Defense, must work very closely with the Department of State and USAID [U.S. Agency for International Development] as they work to support the Iraqi government.

And we must stay committed, we must be working with our international partners. The U.N. is doing quite a bit in Iraq right now on not only the humanitarian assistance issues, but also stabilization. They are doing that under and with the Iraqi government. I think that is important that we support the Iraqi government for their viability, and I think if there is anything a little bit different, we are all focused on supporting that government, that Iraqi security force, and working holistically from our government.

And to answer your question, we absolutely need to work more closely and support our State colleagues on what the needs are, what the whole needs are for that long term.

Mr. MOULTON. Thank you, Mr. Swayne. I mean, I am pleased to hear that, because earlier you had said that the DOD effort is to defeat ISIS and that was it. We need a whole-of-government approach.

Mr. SWAYNE. No, sir. And I apologize if we didn't—I didn't have my opening remarks. I didn't get to——

Mr. MOULTON. Fair enough.

Mr. SWAYNE [continuing]. Say those points. So I had to go back and review those and get that. But there is no doubt about it. It is a whole-of-government approach.

Mr. MOULTON. Madam Chairwoman, thank you very much.

Mr. SWAYNE. I apologize if I——

Mr. MOULTON. Thank you.

Mrs. HARTZLER. Thank you. Representative Banks, Indiana.

Mr. BANKS. Thank you, Madam Chair.

Mr. Pennington, can you talk a little bit about the security cooperation budget for Iraq in a post-ISIS environment? What does that budget look like today? What are the strategies for what that budget might look like tomorrow moving forward?

Mr. PENNINGTON. Congressman, I know there have been discussions between others from the administration, from the Department about budget issues, and I am not really prepared to talk about specifics of the budget.

We have a robust security cooperation program with Iraq through foreign military financing [FMF] that I know the subcommittee is aware of. We are continuing that. There is also a train-and-equip element to this that is DOD-run that my colleagues may wish to comment on. But in terms of what budgets look like going forward, I think we need to leave that to other briefers.

Mr. BANKS. So is it safe to assume, though, that the FMF budget might look different in a post-ISIS environment than what it does today?

Mr. PENNINGTON. Congressman, I am just not in a position to say what it is going to look like.

Mr. BANKS. Okay, that is disappointing. Thank you. I yield back.

Mrs. HARTZLER. Representative Gallego.

Mr. GALLEGO. Mr. Swayne, why isn't the OSD [Office of the Secretary of Defense] Policy's Middle East office or the office of the ASD [Assistant Secretary of Defense] for International Security Affairs presented here or presenting here today?

Mr. SWAYNE. Thank you, sir. My office was asked to come represent—because my area of specialty is stabilization and humanitarian assistance. And it was determined that the aim of this particular committee, subcommittee discussion would be to focus in that post-ISIS—what we can look to do, the Department of Defense supporting other interagencies in that area. That is the reason, sir.

Mr. GALLEGO. Okay. Interesting. Is there a disagreement in policy or is there a lack of engagement, in your opinion, by the regional office leadership at the Pentagon on ISIL's life cycle, especially post-Mosul? We just actually had another briefing before this discussing this, also.

Mr. SWAYNE. No, sir. I see no lack of—we are certainly coherent in policy. I think that is—they feel comfortable that they can send somebody besides the DASD [Deputy Assistant Secretary of Defense] for Middle East up here to brief on our activities. When we talked about the last question by Congressman Banks was to talk about the—what is the budget for the Department of Defense 2017, we have $1.1 billion for the training and equipping through NDAA [National Defense Authorization Act] section 1236 authority, and in 2018, we are planned $1.27 billion.

So it is certainly as the number of dollars and our commitment to working with the Iraqi security forces, not lessening, it is increasing, we certainly see the need—again, as we talked about we have a plan to defeat ISIS, but the seeds of the next resurgence of ISIS are in the rubble of where the ISIS-controlled areas right now, the areas that ISIS destroyed, and we need to be diligent and work closely with the Iraqi security forces, working with our interagency partners, as we sustain that stability so that ISIS 2.0 doesn't grow out of those seeds that are in the rubble.

So we are certainly committed to it, Congressman.

Mr. GALLEGO. Thank you, Mr. Swayne. Who is the acting or current—or who is the current DASD for the Middle East?

Mr. SWAYNE. Yes, sir. The current DASD for—is an acting DASD——

Mr. GALLEGO. Acting.

Mr. SWAYNE [continuing]. Brigadier general rank. I believe that is also another reason we have two—we would have two military uniformed officers up here. And I felt that—I believe the leadership felt that it would more appropriate if a civilian representative of OSD Policy—brigadier general rank is certainly in tune with all of these activities. I talk to him every day about Iraq, Syria, and the de-ISIS efforts.

Thank you, sir.

Mr. GALLEGO. Just in closing, Madam Chair and Ranking Member, I think it is—for me, it shows a certain level of disagreement and also lack of commitment when we have so many acting positions that are being filled in a policy area that we all think is extremely important.

Thank you. I yield back my time.

Mrs. HARTZLER. Thank you. Representative Scott.

Mr. SCOTT. Thank you, Madam Chair. General, you talked about, if you will, a unifying enemy that has brought people together. Assuming that we are able to defeat that enemy in the near future, one of the issues that will have to be addressed is the issue of the Kurds.

They have recently had an overwhelming referendum on independence. And my question revolves around that. How do you see stability in the region for the Kurds after the defeat of ISIS?

General BIERMAN. You would agree with me, sir, it is a very concerning development. It is one we tried to forestall across the whole of government. Secondary to the political and diplomatic interactions we had with the KRG [Kurdistan Regional Government] leadership, we certainly messaged that at the military level, as well.

It has occurred now. You know, the referendum has come and gone. And we are watching that very, very closely. One of the key factors in the battlefield successes that we have had against ISIL in Iraq has been Kurdish and Iraqi security forces cooperating and working together, most recently demonstrated in the liberation of Mosul.

And we can't afford to have this referendum and whatever follows destabilize us as we are on the brink of defeating physical ISIS. We are watching events very, very closely on the ground. There has been some political maneuvering that is occurring.

So far, we have not seen any elevation of violence, but, you know, secondary to what is going on, on the diplomatic side, we certainly in the military are messaging both Iraqi and Kurdish military leaders that we have established very strong relationships with over the last couple years. It is a concern.

Mr. SCOTT. What are Iran's intentions in Iraq and Syria? I mean, do they intend to just try to continue to foster chaos? What do you think the end game for Iran is?

General BIERMAN. I think the Iranians want to ensure that they create conditions in Iraq so that they are never threatened like they were during the 1980s, which was a horrific and bloody war, and both countries suffered significantly.

I think the Iranians want to establish a land bridge that goes from Tehran all the way into areas of Syria and Lebanon where they can threaten and potentially apply pressure to Israel. But I think ultimately I would walk back to the first of my answer and say the Iranians seek a neighboring Iraq which cannot threaten the revolution and the Iranian regime.

Mr. SCOTT. Madam Chair, I know we are short on time. I will yield the remainder of my time so that other members can ask questions, as well.

Mrs. HARTZLER. Thank you very much, and those were very good questions on Kurds and Iran. Representative O'Halleran.

Mr. O'HALLERAN. Thank you, Madam Chairwoman.

General, thank you for your service to our country. You had mentioned a fragile government. What defines that fragile government? And in your mind, what can we do to change that?

General BIERMAN. Yes, sir, I want to make sure I stay in my lane, but I think Iraq is a country made up of a lot of very different, disparate cultural, religious, demographic elements. During my five trips back and forth to Iraq, I have been in Shia land, I have been in the Sunni areas, and I have been in Kurdistan. And I think it is a tremendous challenge to any government to try to knit together people with those kind of different interests and agendas, and then to provide responsible and inclusive governance.

I would, sir, go back to what I said before at the risk maybe of repeating myself a little bit. We are very, very focused on ensuring that our efforts to enable the Iraqi security forces, you know, address any internal or external threat, that that buys the time for the Iraqi government to continue to coalesce, improve, and provide that responsible governance to the people of Iraq.

Mr. O'HALLERAN. Thank you, General. Luckily, we have Mr. Pennington here. And if you can expand on that question and also identify what the current staffing levels are in Iraq for the State Department. Are there additional needs that you look into—have? And what are the funding levels for assistance into the area?

Mr. PENNINGTON. Thank you, Congressman. On the question of governance and fragility of governance, I think it is fair to say that the United States government has been very actively engaged in trying to shore up the Iraqi government on a number of fronts. I mentioned the support for Iraqi priorities of humanitarian assistance and stabilization of liberated areas. That is the prime minister's focus. That is what helps him politically and helps the government strengthen institutionally.

I would also point out the support that we have provided to the Iraqi government in terms of getting its fiscal house in order on the economic side. The economic pressures that Iraq has been under, because of the conflict, the presence of ISIS, the collapse of oil prices, the humanitarian crisis, that created an economic crisis both in Baghdad and Irbil of massive proportions.

We and other G–7 [Group of Seven] partners stepped forward to fill the fiscal gap. We through a sovereign loan guarantee, a $1 billion sovereign loan guarantee, which the Iraqis then followed up by borrowing in the private market, that would not have been possible without our support. And getting a deal with the IMF [International Monetary Fund], which provided the additional financing necessary to close that gap and keep the government on its feet during this time of tremendous challenge, again, would not have been possible without U.S. support.

And that—the IMF program has been the key to starting the government on a path of significant economic reform, which they are complying with the conditions of the IMF program. So on all of those fronts, we are being both responsive to the needs, the political needs of the Iraqi leadership, supporting them where it is most important to them, and also strengthening the institutions.

Mr. O'HALLERAN. And do you feel that the staffing levels are adequate and that—the funding levels, are the question I asked.

Mr. PENNINGTON. Congressman, in terms of staffing, there was a decline in staffing following the incursion of ISIS into Iraq for security reasons. A lot of those numbers have now trended back up. The chief of mission has—is continually making recommendations on staffing levels to respond to needs that he sees on the ground. Washington has been fully responsive to those requests, and so we work those issues on a daily, weekly basis.

Mr. O'HALLERAN. And funding?

Mr. PENNINGTON. Funding, in terms of our economic support funding for Iraq, has been holding steady. We are well resourced for this year for the activities that I described. Again, not going to get into a discussion of budget levels going forward, but we think for the moment we have what we need, particularly when you factor in that coalition partners on the civilian side and support—actually the ratio is roughly 3 to 1. For every dollar we put up for stabilization, humanitarian efforts, our coalition partners come up with about three times that. And so put all that together, and I think the support has been quite robust.

Mr. O'HALLERAN. Thank you, Madam Chair. I yield.

Mrs. HARTZLER. Thank you. Representative Panetta.

Mr. PANETTA. Thank you, Madam Chair. Lady and gentlemen, thank you very much for being here. Appreciate your testimony, your preparation, obviously.

I admit you know a heck of a lot more about this topic than I do. And so my question is going to be pretty broad and pretty easy. But I think in order to accomplish a lot of the goals that you are talking about, you not only need money, you not only need military help and diplomacy, but you need credibility. And so based on your experience, what is the United States reputation in Iraq with the government, with the people? And does that affect our ability to accomplish our mission?

Mr. PENNINGTON. Maybe I will start, Congressman. That is a great question. I will be happy to start, but I would welcome other comments.

I think we have built up since the incursion of ISIS, the coming to power of the Abadi government in summer of 2014, and the way that the military and now subsequently the humanitarian, the support has played out in Iraq, I think there is a recognition that the United States role has been indispensable in allowing Iraq to make the progress that it has made. And I think it is hard to quantify in terms of public support, but I think what we do see is a broad spectrum of support across sectarian lines in Iraq that understand the benefits of an America—of a strong relationship with the United States and American presence. And this goes Shia, Sunni, Kurd.

And so when we talk about a future relationship, whether it is security, economic partnership, commercial relationship, I think it is safe to say that there is broad support across the Iraqi political spectrum. And I believe that does translate at the popular level, as well. It is harder to measure.

Mr. PANETTA. Despite what happened, you know, after 2003, what happened with the Iraq war?

Mr. PENNINGTON. I think our absence from Iraq or our pulling back from Iraq in 2011, for all—and that is another topic that we probably won't get into here today—but it did—and then our coming back to Iraq in a sense in 2014, when Iraq was faced with the most grave crisis, has really I think changed minds in Iraq or—of course, there are some who will never accept that presence. But I think most Iraqis want the U.S. to be with them, want our support, welcome our support, and look for a long-term relationship with the United States.

General BIERMAN. I would just, sir, add to that good answer by saying we have gained a level of credibility in the way we have conducted the campaign. You know, looking back at where we were at 2014, when ISIS had overrun much of western and northern Iraq, working by, with, and through the Iraqi security forces, we have steadily over a period of 2 years, we have stayed focused, we have stayed committed, we have made common cause with the Iraqis, and we are seen in some respects as winners.

But I would say—and, you know, it is a soft pat on the back if at all—that is not going to be enough in the long term. And one of the drumbeat themes from all of you is, it needs to be political and it needs to be diplomatic. And I think we could very easily lose some of the credibility we have gained by battlefield military success if we don't translate those gains into stabilization, you know, still a million displaced Sunnis who—they think it is great that their city has been liberated, but if their homes, their neighborhoods, their infrastructure is wrecked, whatever goodwill time we have bought for the Iraqi government, we have got to follow up on that rapidly. And that is going to be a big determinant of our long-term credibility.

Mr. SWAYNE. My answer to that question, Congressman, is in the past after 2003 we were the—I would put it in the terms of we were the big brother and we had a little brother in the last few years. It is a partnership. They have an established government.

They have an established Iraqi security force. We are not the big brother. We are a partner along with other coalition members who are coming in working with side by side. I think that is also a bit of a difference that it is not this paternalistic relationship. It is a specific.

Mr. PANETTA. Thank you, Madam Chair. I yield back.

Mrs. HARTZLER. Thank you. Representative Suozzi.

Mr. SUOZZI. Thank you, Madam Chairwoman. Thank you to all of you for your service to our country. We are very grateful to you for your good work.

I traveled to Afghanistan in the spring, and there was a very clear military five-point plan as to what the strategy was going to be from a military perspective. And I am certain that there is a clear military strategy that has been documented by the Department of Defense related to Iraq and Syria.

My question is, does the Department of State have a good document that I can read as to what the long-term plan is over the next 4 or 5 years related to both Afghanistan and Iraq and Syria? Ms. Quanrud? No?

Mr. PENNINGTON. Thank you, sir. Just to clarify. Are we talking on the military side?

Mr. SUOZZI. No, on the Department of State side, on more the civilian side.

Mr. PENNINGTON. We do have a—we have had strategy documents that are not time-limited that define our interests and long-term strategies in Iraq. Afghanistan is outside of, I think, any of our purview. Those are things we could discuss in a different setting.

Mr. SUOZZI. Okay, but I would like to get that document, if I can. Give me a good document to read. Okay?

Mr. PENNINGTON. We will take that back.

Mr. SUOZZI. Thank you. I yield back my time.

Mrs. HARTZLER. Thank you. Just wondering, how many of you have read the testimony from the first panel before? Have you had access to that or have you had an opportunity? Raise your hand if you have. You have. Good, good. I thought it had a lot of good suggestions, a lot of good insights to be considered in there. So I am glad to hear that you did that.

General, there was some discussion in the last panel about the number of troops that we should have remain to stabilize once ISIS is defeated. Do you have an opinion on that? What do you think that we need, as far as numbers of troops?

General BIERMAN. Yes, ma'am. And I know you will understand if I talk probably generally without specific numbers. We want to ensure that there is a balance that we need to strike. Coming back to the discussion of plans, our focus after the defeat of ISIS in terms of reliable partnership, building Iraqi capacity, is going to be on training, equipping, intelligence, counterterrorism, and security assistance.

And I would say we want to leave just enough, but we also need to ensure that we remain very aware of the Iraqi political environment and that we don't wear out our welcome. The Iraqis continue to signal that we want us there, and we are having some very positive talks in terms of what is the right amount.

There was a comment made earlier about some of the resource challenges we are seeing with all our commitments across the globe. So we are very focused on what is the smallest amount that we can leave in terms of residual capacity that will have the effect that we need to build Iraqi capacity.

I think the conversations which are not in our lane, but we are a part of have been very positive back-and-forth between U.S., Iraqi governments, and some of the participating coalition governments.

Mrs. HARTZLER. Mr. Pennington, along those lines, one of the most important things that needs to occur is this political solution. It is the very difficult job of putting together an inclusive government that has Sunni and Shia and Kurds and is going to, you know, respect all the minorities, Christians, Yazidis, et cetera.

What efforts are being made by the Department of State now to help force this discussion and this relationship? And with the presence of Iran there, how successful do you think this would be, to be able to get this together and get it right?

Mr. PENNINGTON. Thank you, Madam Chairwoman. Again, we are now heading into an Iraqi election season, so these issues are going to be debated during the course of that process. We can't, of course, control how that process comes out, but we can, of course, make sure that we are in connection with those across the spectrum in pushing them toward our central ideas of how governance—how we see governance in Iraq, which is inclusive, which is responsive, which is service-oriented, and which is cognizant of all sects, including minorities and their interests.

So we have discussions with all sides, Sunni, Shia, Kurd minority across the spectrum about those issues. They know that support from the United States depends on inclusive governance. We have made that very, very clear. We see the prime minister as someone who is governing Iraq from—and despite all the challenges, from a nationalist, from an Iraqi perspective, not from a sectarian perspective.

And so we see that he has developed, we believe, support from populations including many of the communities who have been liberated, which are mostly Sunni communities. And so the—if you look at public opinion polling in Iraq, for example, the attitudes toward the central government in Baghdad among Sunni populations have increased significantly in the last 6 to 12 months, because of the effort against ISIS and the effort to get people to return to their homes.

And so we definitely have influence on the process and on the actors, but in the end, these are Iraqi political decisions. There will be coalitions formed, alliances formed. Our preference, of course, is that those alliances include cross-sectarian groupings. We think that in the current environment that that is possible and even likely.

Mrs. HARTZLER. Very good, thank you. Do you have any secondary questions? Yes, Representative Moulton.

Mr. MOULTON. Just a concluding comment. And I want to, first of all, thank you all for participating in the panel. Just as I expressed the responsibility that I feel as a member of this committee, but especially as an Iraq war veteran, to ensure that we don't waste more lives in Iraq, that we finally get this right after many times of getting it wrong and repeating our same mistakes, I hope you will feel that responsibility, as well.

And I know that it is difficult working under an administration and having the constraints of that environment, where not everybody in the administration may see eye to eye with you or may agree with you. But I hope that you will remember the troops on the ground, the State Department folks on the ground, the people who are trying to get this right and need your support to succeed.

Thank you.

Mr. SWAYNE. Congressman, can I just make a point about that?

Mr. MOULTON. Yes, sir.

Mr. SWAYNE. I pledged my allegiance to the Constitution, and I support the President of the United States and all the people appointed over me, but I come to work every day because of all the soldiers, sailors, airmen, and marines that are out there, and also our State Department people. So I take that commitment to heart.

And I think we would be remiss if we didn't acknowledge that we are deeply saddened, but on October 1st, just most recently in Iraq, a service member lost his life to an IED [improvised explosive device]. Another service men was a casualty to that. So our heartfelt condolences go out to their families. And that is not lost on me or anybody on the panel. So we appreciate you saying that, and we certainly think about it, sir.

Mr. MOULTON. Thank you, Mr. Swayne.

Mrs. HARTZLER. I just wanted to thank each of you for coming today. And thank you for your commitment to the issue at hand and getting Iraq—having an opportunity to have success there for the future and remembering the troops. I think we have lost—over 4,500 American soldiers have given their lives to give the people of Iraq an opportunity to have freedom and to keep us safe here at home.

And so thank you for remembering that every day and for keeping that in mind. I am encouraged by the polling and some of the things we are seeing, the gains that have been made the last few years. But we need to make sure and get this right moving forward.

We have a wonderful opportunity ahead of us to chart a new path for Iraq. It is not going to be easy, but I know us here in Congress and on this committee are committed to doing what we can to help support this effort, because we want to see it succeed from here on out.

And so we appreciate your commitment to that, look forward to working with you, and thank you for coming today, for your testimony. And with that, our hearing is adjourned.

[Whereupon, at 5:31 p.m., the subcommittee was adjourned.]

APPENDIX

October 3, 2017

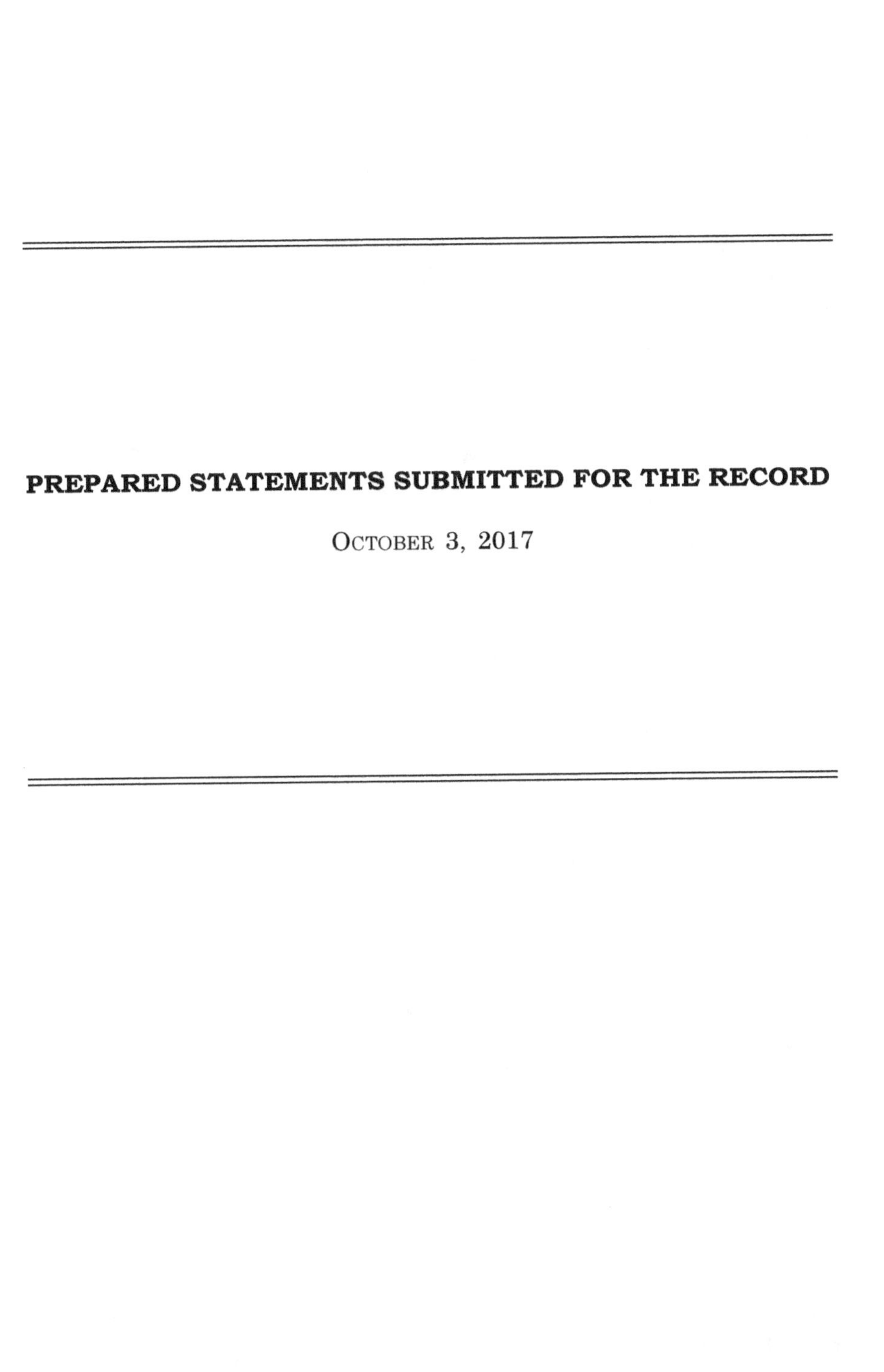

PREPARED STATEMENTS SUBMITTED FOR THE RECORD

OCTOBER 3, 2017

Opening Remarks of Chairwoman Vicky Hartzler
Subcommittee on Oversight & Investigations Hearing
"Securing the Peace After the Fall of ISIL"

October 3, 2017

Good afternoon. This hearing will come to order.

Welcome to our subcommittee members and witnesses testifying before us today.

We convene today to consider how the United States intends to secure the peace once ISIL is defeated.

This is a very important issue to the Committee, to this subcommittee, and to me, to Ranking Member Moulton, and to other Members. It is essential and appropriate that we exercise proper oversight as our country's plans are formulated and funding is authorized.

Following Operation Iraqi Freedom, the United States worked to re-establish civil institutions and rebuild the military and police forces in Iraq. Nonetheless, conditions in the country deteriorated, leaving a security void that ISIL managed to exploit. We owe it to our men and women in uniform to learn lessons from that experience so that history does not repeat itself. It is critical that we do all we can here in Congress to ensure a stable Iraq after ISIL is defeated. Today's hearing will offer Members an opportunity to learn more about how the Administration intends to achieve success beyond the battlefield.

Our first panel of very insightful outside experts will discuss the broader strategic issues associated with ISIL's loss of territory, and highlight critical issues that should be considered as the Administration's Iraq policy evolves. Our second panel today will address the numerous challenges associated with stabilization and rebuilding in Iraq and discuss the status of US government efforts to improve the political and security environment in Iraq.

Ranking Member Moulton Opening Remarks
House Armed Services Committee Subcommittee on Oversight &
Investigations
Hearing on "Securing the Peace After the Fall of ISIL"

October 3, 2017

Thank you, Chairwoman Hartzler and thank you to all of our witnesses.

Today, the subcommittee will focus on the critically important task of securing the peace in Iraq after the defeat of ISIS. I echo Chairwoman Hartzler's frustration in securing appropriate administration witnesses to answer the full gamut of questions the Oversight and Investigations Subcommittee is within its purview to raise but am grateful for everyone's presence here today and ongoing service to our country.

I also appreciate our outside witnesses who bring considerable depth of expertise to bear on this subject, including Amb. Crocker who I first met in Iraq while serving under Gen. David Petraeus.

As we convene here today, Iraqi security forces, supported by the U.S. advise and assist mission have succeeded in retaking most major population centers once controlled by ISIS—Falluja, Ramadi, and Mosul, ISIS' power center in Iraq. Most recently, coalition supported Iraqi Forces seized back the city Tal Afar in the northwestern corner of Iraq and only isolated ISIS strongholds remain outside of Hawija, Qaim, and other pockets along the Syria-Iraq border.

Such victories have not been without a human toll. ISIS' brutal tactics, employing civilians as human shields, vehicle-borne improvised explosive devices, and booby-trapped residential areas resulted in over 1,400 Iraqi troops killed and at least 7,000 wounded according to our embassy in Baghdad. During the campaign, two American servicemembers were killed and over 20 were wounded.

The U.S. Commander of the Combined Joint Task Force in charge of the counter-ISIS campaign, Lt. Gen. Stephen Townsend, called it "worst fighting he had seen in 35 years" of combat experience and likened it to "Falluja 2004 on steroids."

Civilian losses have been greater still, with latest UN estimates at 8,000 killed and 1.2 million rendered homeless, displaced by the fighting.
Despite the tragic human toll, I am encouraged by the progress we have made in partnership with Iraqi forces to defeat the scourge of ISIS and look forward to hearing from our witnesses an update on the final stages of the military campaign.

As important and necessary as these operations are to militarily defeat ISIS, I am concerned that without sufficient post-conflict planning and resourcing we will find ourselves and Iraqi forces condemned to fighting the same battles so many have already given their lives for.

At its core, what troubles Iraq are fundamentally political questions. Just as I disagreed with the Obama administration, I am again concerned this administration is not sufficiently prioritizing such underlying political dynamics.

What does this mean? First and foremost, I am concerned Iraqi security forces may be woefully unprepared to provide security to Iraqi civilians and ensure displaced persons can return to their homes without fear of attack or retribution. Experts I have heard from here in Washington and in Iraq have expressed worries of insufficient hold forces and police, compounded by the beleaguered state of Iraqi military units, reeling from the toll of the brutal counter-ISIS campaign.

Without sufficient local security arrangements, we cannot expect for Iraq to be stabilized, for civilians return to normalcy, and for communities to be defended against the emergence of an "ISIS 2.0" or other militant groups. Moreover, without capable and professional security forces, we risk seeing a repeat of the same sectarian tensions leading to Sunni embitterment that provided fertile ground for the growth of ISIS.

Beyond the provisioning of civilian security, key gaps and problems remain to be addressed such as acute food insecurity, insufficient access to healthcare, destroyed infrastructure, degraded public services and utilities, newly inflamed grievances among local communities, and insufficient plans for governance arrangements in many areas.

Both as a Marine infantry officer who worked side-by-side with Iraqis to turn the tide of the insurgency and now as a Congressman and Ranking Member of this Oversight and Investigations Subcommittee, I look forward to your testimony, and hope to hear a proactive, whole-of-government strategy that represents the only chance of success.

I cannot tell you how painful it is as an Iraq war veteran to see us fighting and re-fighting the same battles we fought and for which our friends gave their lives. At this rate, my children will be fighting these same battles.

We must hear from the administration how this time will be different, how this time you will ensure a political resolution so that the U.S. military doesn't have to keep cleaning up these messes.

Thank you, Chairwoman Hartzler, I yield back.

Testimony of Ryan Crocker before the House Armed Services Committee Subcommittee on Oversight and Investigations
September 12, 2017
Room 2212 Rayburn House Office Building

Madam Chairwoman, Ranking Member Moulton, members of the Subcommittee, It is a great honor to testify before you on a matter of vital concern for our national security, the need to secure the peace after the fall of ISIL.

The military defeat of ISIL is assured. It is a question of time, and people of the region have been asking themselves for the past year or more a fundamental question: then what? Iraqis and Syrians have understood for some time that what happens after ISIL's defeat may be more important than the defeat itself.

It is roughly a century since the modern middle east was created from the rubble of the Ottoman Empire. The region has witnessed turmoil throughout this period, but nothing on the scale of what we see today. Coups and revolutions always have been part of the landscape. But what we are seeing today is the collapse of states and the parallel rise of non-state actors such as ISIL. In this sense, ISIL is the symptom of a deeply rooted problem, not the problem itself. That problem is a chronic failure of governance.

Another way to look at the issue as a failure of isms, beginning with imperialism. The French and British, who divided the region between them at Versaille in 1919, had no interest in the development of stable institutions, respect for the rule of law or the preparation of the peoples of their for self-governance. The United States, on the other hand, was focused on precisely those issues through the report of the King-Crane Commission in 1919 which recommended that the sole purpose of a mandate should be to prepare the people of the region for self-determination. It recommended a single mandate held by the United States for a finite period. The Commission's report never saw daylight, and the rest, as they say, is history.

Other isms followed: monarchism in countries like Iraq, Egypt and Libya where links to the mandatory powers compromised their legitimacy, Arab nationalism personified by Nasser in Egypt, Arab socialism (Baathism) in Iraq and Syria, communism in south Yemen, and undiluted authoritarianism followed. All failed to provide good governance and its benefits. Now we are witnessing the emergence of yet another ism, Islamism. It too will fail, and it too has failed to provide good governance. Interestingly, ISIL seemed to understand this during its brief ascendancy seeking to take over health clinics in Syria and projecting a focus on rule of law in Mosul. These efforts soon fell by the wayside, victims of coalition pressure and ISIL's own extremist ideology.

When I was ambassador to Iraq from 2007 - 2009, a key coalition and Iraqi government priority during the surge was the elimination of Al Qaida in Iraq, the predecessor of ISIL. We could never quite get there. Small pockets remained, in Mosul and and up the Euphrates river valley. Why? Elements of the Sunni population feared the Shia - led Iraqi government more than they feared AQI. This was at a time when significant progress had been made toward stabilizing the country politically as well as militarily, Sunnis had rejoined the political process, and a second provincial council election left defeated incumbents crying fraud, but also cleaning out their desks and vowing to do better next time.

Conditions are far less propitious now. Budget shortfalls have severely impacted reconstruction efforts in predominantly Sunni cities. Our absence has been filled by an Iranian presence, both direct and indirect through the activities of Iranian backed Shia militias over which the Iraqi government has very little control. These are not circumstances favorable to the establishment of good governance.

I understand that the American people are tired of US involvement in distant wars that consume blood and treasure and that seem to have no end. I understand that. I have spent seven years since 9/11 in Iraq, Pakistan and Afghanistan, so I know what tiredness feels like. But there are worse things than being tired. These are issues that directly affect our national security.

I learned several lessons very painfully in the middle east. They are simple but have profound impact. One is be careful what you get into. Military interventions in the region have major and extended consequences, consequences of not just of the third and fourth order but of the thirtieth and fortieth order. I learned this not in Iraq but in Lebanon when I was posted to Beirut in the early 1980s including the Israeli invasion of 1982. It is widely believed that the US gave a silent nod to the Israeli plans. And who could argue with the aim of ending Palestinian terror attacks across the Israeli-Palestinian border? But the consequences were enormous. This was the catalyst for a strategic partnership between Syria and the new Islamic Republic that endures to this day. Out of that partnership came Hizballah and its precursors, far more deadly than the PLO ever was. I am a survivor of the April 1983 bombing of the American Embassy in Beirut, and was present when the Marine barracks were blown up six months later. We often speak of intelligence failures. I tend to see most such instances as failures not of intelligence but of imagination. We are unable to imagine such unintended consequences.

When I arrived in Baghdad in March 2007, I had the eerie feeling of being transported back to Beirut a quarter of a century earlier. The same antagonists, Iran and Syria, were inflicting pain on us with the same instruments. The lesson they absorbed from Lebanon was that if you cause them pain, the Americans will leave. And it almost worked.

The other lesson I learned, therefore, is that if we need to be careful about what we get into, we need to be at least as careful over what we get out of. Disengagement can have consequences as profound and unpredictable as those set in motion by one's initial intervention. One does not end wars by withdrawing one's troops. That simply cedes the battle space to adversaries more determined and more patient, in this case to Iran and its proxies and to ISIL.

Let me say something about Iran. Some in this country believe that cooperation with Iran in confronting ISIL is possible and desirable. It is neither. Iran does not feel threatened by ISIL. They do see it as a valuable justification for actions such as the formation of the Popular Mobilization Units which are controlled by Tehran much more than by Baghdad. These units are potentially a greater threat to Iraqi stability and our interests than ISIL was. I would suggest to you that Iran's main strategic goal in Iraq is to insure that whoever rules in Baghdad will never again be able to threaten Iran's existence as Saddam did when he invaded Iraq in 1980. Few in this country remember that horrific eight year conflict; even fewer in Iran and Iraq will ever forget it.

So what do we do to secure the peace after ISIL is defeated? First, we need to understand this is in its essence a political problem, not a military one. There are some security issues on which there is remarkable continuity between the Trump and Obama Administrations. Unfortunately, one of them is treating ISIL only as a security issue. When the last bastion of ISIL falls, I fear we will declare our work in Iraq and Syria done. The reality is that it is the beginning of a complex political process, not its end. I very much hope that we will realize that US leadership is essential for any prospect of long term stability in Iraq. We need to make that commitment, much as the President did recently with Afghanistan. This need not involve the dispatch of substantial numbers of additional US forces. It does mean the need to signal that Iraq is a presidential level priority. It would mean substantial engagement by the Secretary of State with Iraqi leaders, with regional states and with the international community, and this engagement will need to be maintained for an indefinite period of time. We have the Strategic Framework Agreement signed by President Bush and Prime Minister Maliki in 2008 as a framework to work within. The agreement lays out the principles of US - Iraqi cooperation in a wide variety of fields, and we should use it as a guide for a long term relationship with Baghdad.

None of this is easy and it certainly won't be quick. But perceptions of US disengagement during the Obama Administration has not brought Iraq or the region to a better place. A century ago, a US withdrawal from the world effectively produced a two decade truce in one long world war and set the stage for the disfunction we are now witnessing in the middle east. The US did exercise a global leadership role after World War II, and it was that leadership over seven decades that brought about the collapse of the Soviet Union and prevented another global conflagration. The world is not yet ready to run by itself.

I have focused my attention primarily on Iraq where a political process is not only possible but necessary. Syria is clearly not at that point. It is a fire that will burn for some time to come, and we certainly need to do what we can to contain it. But the day when political solutions are feasible is far from dawning.

With our sustained commitment, and that of regional and international allies, the Iraqis may be able to achieve a degree of political and economic inclusion that will produce long term stability. Developments since our disengagement in 2001 make painfully clear that they will not get there on their own. Just as the absence of good governance fueled the rise of ISIL as Al Qaida in Iraq version 2.0, so too will it lead to the emergence of something we cannot yet imagine. To paraphrase the great Irish poet William Butler Yeats, what rough beast, its hour come at last, slouches toward Baghdad to be born?

Madam Chairwoman, Ranking Member Moulton, members of the Subcommittee, I thank you again for the privilege of testifying before you today.

Ryan Crocker

Ryan Crocker is a Diplomat in Residence at the Woodrow Wilson School, Princeton University, for the academic year 2017-2018. He is on a leave of absence as an executive professor at Texas A&M University where he served as dean of the Bush School of Government & Public Service until August 2016. He also has had appointments as the James Schlesinger Distinguished Visiting Professor at the University of Virginia and as the first Kissinger Senior Fellow at Yale University.

He retired from the Foreign Service in April 2009 after a career of over 37 years but was recalled to active duty by President Obama to serve as U.S. Ambassador to Afghanistan in 2011. He has served as U.S. Ambassador six times: Afghanistan (2011-2012), Iraq (2007-2009), Pakistan (2004-2007), Syria (1998-2001), Kuwait (1994-1997), and Lebanon (1990-1993).   He has also served as the International Affairs Advisor at the National War College, where he joined the faculty in 2003. From May to August 2003, he was in Baghdad as the first Director of Governance for the Coalition Provisional Authority and was Deputy Assistant Secretary of State for Near Eastern Affairs from August 2001 to May 2003. Since joining the Foreign Service in 1971, he also has had assignments in Iran, Qatar, Iraq and Egypt, as well as Washington. He was assigned to the American Embassy in Beirut during the Israeli invasion of Lebanon in 1982 and the bombings of the embassy and the Marine barracks in 1983.

Born in Spokane, Washington, he grew up in an Air Force family, attending schools in Morocco, Canada and Turkey, as well as the U.S. He received a B.A. in English in 1971 and an honorary Doctor of Laws degree in 2001 from Whitman College (Washington). He also holds an honorary Doctorate in National Security Affairs from the National Defense University (2010), honorary Doctor of Laws degrees from Gonzaga University (2009) and Seton Hall University (2012), as well as an honorary Doctor of Humane Letters degree from the American University of Afghanistan (2013). He is a member of the Council on Foreign Relations, the American Academy of Diplomacy, and the Association of American Ambassadors. In August 2013, he was confirmed by the United States Senate to serve on the Broadcasting Board of Governors which oversees all U.S. government-supported civilian international media. He is also on the Board of Directors for Mercy Corps International and is a Trustee of the Rockefeller Brothers Fund.

Ambassador Crocker received the Presidential Medal of Freedom, the nation's highest civilian award, in 2009. His other awards include the Presidential Distinguished and Meritorious Service Awards, the Secretary of State's Distinguished Service Award (2008 and 2012), the Department of Defense Medal for Distinguished Civilian Service (1997 and 2008) and for Distinguished Public Service (2012), the Award for Valor and the American Foreign Service Association Rivkin Award for creative dissent. He received the National Clandestine Service's Donovan Award in 2009 and the Director of Central Intelligence's Director's Award in 2012. In 2011, he was awarded the Marshall Medal by the Association of the United States Army. In January 2002, he was sent to Afghanistan to reopen the American Embassy in Kabul. He subsequently received the Robert C. Frasure Memorial Award for "exceptional courage and leadership" in Afghanistan. In September 2004, President Bush conferred on him the personal rank of Career Ambassador, the highest in the Foreign Service. In May 2009, Secretary of State Hillary Clinton announced the establishment of the Ryan C. Crocker Award for Outstanding Achievement in Expeditionary Diplomacy. In July 2012, he was named an Honorary Marine, the 75th civilian so honored in the history of the Corps.

DISCLOSURE FORM FOR WITNESSES
COMMITTEE ON ARMED SERVICES
U.S. HOUSE OF REPRESENTATIVES

INSTRUCTION TO WITNESSES: Rule 11, clause 2(g)(5), of the Rules of the U.S. House of Representatives for the 115th Congress requires nongovernmental witnesses appearing before House committees to include in their written statements a curriculum vitae and a disclosure of the amount and source of any federal contracts or grants (including subcontracts and subgrants), or contracts or payments originating with a foreign government, received during the current and two previous calendar years either by the witness or by an entity represented by the witness and related to the subject matter of the hearing. This form is intended to assist witnesses appearing before the House Committee on Armed Services in complying with the House rule. Please note that a copy of these statements, with appropriate redactions to protect the witness's personal privacy (including home address and phone number) will be made publicly available in electronic form not later than one day after the witness's appearance before the committee. Witnesses may list additional grants, contracts, or payments on additional sheets, if necessary.

Witness name: RYAN CROCKER

Capacity in which appearing: (check one)

☒ Individual

☐ Representative

If appearing in a representative capacity, name of the company, association or other entity being represented: ____

Federal Contract or Grant Information: If you or the entity you represent before the Committee on Armed Services has contracts (including subcontracts) or grants (including subgrants) with the federal government, please provide the following information:

2017

Federal grant/ contract	Federal agency	Dollar value	Subject of contract or grant
None			

2016

Foreign contract/ payment	Foreign government	Dollar value	Subject of contract or payment
None			

2015

Foreign contract/ payment	Foreign government	Dollar value	Subject of contract or payment
None			

2016

Federal grant/ contract	Federal agency	Dollar value	Subject of contract or grant
None			

2015

Federal grant/ contract	Federal agency	Dollar value	Subject of contract or grant
None			

Foreign Government Contract or Payment Information: If you or the entity you represent before the Committee on Armed Services has contracts or payments originating from a foreign government, please provide the following information:

2017

Foreign contract/ payment	Foreign government	Dollar value	Subject of contract or payment
None			

Statement before the United States House of Representatives Committee on Armed Services
Subcommittee on Oversight and Investigations
On Securing the Peace After the Fall of ISIL

US Policy Toward Iraq

Kenneth M. Pollack
Resident Scholar

10/3/2017

Madame Chairwoman and distinguished Members, I am honored to be able to appear before you to discuss U.S. policy toward Iraq.

Every year since 2003, knowledgeable Americans have been warning that the current year is absolutely critical in Iraq. They have been right every time and 2018 will be no exception. The next year is likely to see the final defeat of ISIS and national elections that will be crucial as both bellwether and determinant of Iraq's future course. As we look to the next phase of American policy toward Iraq in light of these impending events, we must remember that the United States has made too many mistakes in Iraq in the past, and both Americans and Iraqis have paid too high a price for those mistakes, for us to make yet another.

Iraq remains a complicated country. It's military, bureaucracy, politics, economics, and civil society are all weak, contested, and in desperate need of reform. Its constitution is flawed, in part because of the enforced inclusion of the Kurds in a country where they are a liability, not an asset. It is beset by stronger neighbors seeking to dominate the Iraqi state and manipulate its multiplicity of constituent groups.

Yet all is not lost in Iraq. Indeed, there are many useful building blocks from which to erect a strong new state and society. When I was last in Baghdad this spring, I was struck by how many Iraqis are unhappy about their present, but optimistic about their future. Many are proud of their military forces in defeating ISIS, confident that their upcoming elections will produce a more functional political system, and committed to avoiding another civil war. None of that is a guarantee against future problems, but taken together, it can be a starting point for future progress.

Consequently, U.S. policy toward Iraq after the defeat of ISIS demands close attention and careful planning. It cannot be made up on the fly. It should not be made by tweet. It will not work if done slapdash. However, if it is handled properly, and in close coordination with America's allies in Iraq, elsewhere in the region, and among the wider international community, there is every reason to believe that Iraq can eventually be brought to a stable and peaceful new equilibrium that will allow it to become a force for positive change in the region and a benefit to America's interests. If not, we are likely to find ourselves sucked back into yet another Iraq war.

U.S. Interests in Iraq Today

As always at seminal moments like this, it is important to remind ourselves of what our interests are in Iraq. The first is that we need an Iraq that is stable and at peace—with itself and its neighbors. Because of its location and oil wealth, Iraq remains a critical nation in the Middle East and a critical element of the international economy. Before 2003, a reckless and aggressive Iraq under Saddam Husayn created one set of *external* threats to American interests. After 2003, an endless parade of American mistakes produced reinforcing civil wars that created a different, but equally dangerous set of *internal* threats to U.S. interests.

So peace and stability in Iraq are our paramount interests there. But we need to be careful about what that means. For decades in the Middle East, there has been an addiction to the intertwined notions that "stability" is best achieved by dictatorship, and that dictatorship is therefore the easiest solution to instability. The Arab revolts of 2011 and the instability and civil wars they spawned ought to be sufficient evidence of the fallacy of this idea. Nevertheless, in the specific case of Iraq, it should be understood that autocracy will not create the peace and stability we seek.

For the past century, Iraq has suffered through a staggering list of coups, internal revolts, domestic massacres, and civil wars. Even the totalitarianism and genocidal levels of violence employed by Saddam were not enough to prevent constant internal conflicts—from his many wars with the Kurds (including the 1989 Anfal campaign), to the 1991 Shi'a Intifada, to his violent suppression of Sunni tribes in the 1990s. Since then, we have seen how Nuri al-Maliki's efforts to consolidate autocratic power triggered the ISIS invasion of 2014 and the latest Iraqi civil war.

Instead, ensuring peace and stability in Iraq requires pluralism. Only a democratic system of some kind, one governed by the rule of law and incorporating formidable protections for groups not in power, will reassure Iraq's fractious and fearful communities. Likewise, only a system with a high degree of representation and transparency will ensure that Iraq's economic wealth is equitably distributed, eliminating that as another source of conflict and corruption. In short, when we think about peace and stability in Iraq, it is critical to recognize that both require a pluralist system and while dictatorship might seem like the easier path, it will not get us to where we and the Iraqis need to go. It is a blind alley leading nowhere but back to civil strife.

For that reason, functional pluralism in Iraq must itself be seen as an American objective there, because it is the only realistic way to secure our interest in a peaceful, stable Iraq.

Finally, the United States should seek an Iraq that is not dominated by Iran or Iranian proxies as Lebanon and now Syria increasingly are. At the most obvious level, it would be a humiliation for over 4,500 Americans to have given their lives to make Iraq safe for Iranian dominion. In a more tangible sense, despite repeated American efforts to begin a rapprochement with Iran—including most recently under the Obama Administration—the Iranians continue to define their foreign policy as one of explicit enmity with the United States.

Although Iranian and American interests overlap in important areas despite this, we need to accept that the Iranian regime regards us as their principal adversary and treats us as such. We may not like it. We may wish to change it. We may think it gratuitous or misguided, but we cannot change it. We have tried repeatedly, but the leadership in Tehran is not interested. And as a result, all across the Middle East, Iran aggressively pursues policies harmful to the United States. The Iranian regime is not our friend, and it works hard to do harm to us in a range of venues. We should be loath to see Iraq fall under Tehran's sway.

Moreover, abandoning Iraq to the Iranians would terrify and infuriate our regional allies. The Israelis would be alarmed that Tehran's possession of a contiguous land route from Iran to Lebanon and the Golan Heights would presage new Iranian attacks on Israel—especially once the last embers of resistance to Iran's Syrian ally have been snuffed out. Indeed, the recent Israeli airstrike against Syrian regime bases appear intended to deter and diminish future Syrian-Iranian attacks on Israel as the regime regains control of Syria.

Likewise, the Saudis and other Gulf Arabs would fear that if Iran were allowed to dominate Iraq, it would use Iraqi territory as a base (and Arab Iraqis as agents) to expand its influence, stoke internal unrest, and intimidate them and other Sunni-dominated Arab states like Jordan and Egypt. In the past, we have consistently seen that when our Gulf Arab allies feel threatened by Iran and fear that the United States is not adequately protecting them, they generally overreact and take aggressive actions themselves. In many cases, like the GCC intervention in Yemen since 2015, they lack the capability to execute the missions they take on, making the situation far worse, rather than better. Especially at this moment, when it is so important to American interests that Saudi Arabia and other Arab states concentrate their resources and energy on domestic reforms, we cannot afford to create potentially ruinous external distractions.

Walking away from Iraq to risk renewed internal conflict and/or Iranian domination could only be a tragic, and utterly unnecessary mistake for the United States, especially when we have just achieved so much and could use this opportunity to do so much more to secure American interests in the Middle East.

U.S.-Iraqi Security Assistance after ISIS

As this committee understands well, fashioning a future American policy toward Iraq has to begin with security cooperation and an enduring American military commitment. President Trump was absolutely correct when he argued that the withdrawal of American troops from Iraq in 2011 was a critical element in Iraq's slide back into civil war with the ISIS invasion of 2014. His Administration cannot afford to make the same mistake all over again.

Accordingly, even after the defeat of ISIS, the United States should aim to retain a considerable military mission in Iraq, ideally on the order of at least 10,000 troops. Truth be told, going back to General Lloyd Austin's plan to retain 20,000-25,000 troops would be better still, although I recognize that that may be a bridge too far for both Washington and Baghdad.

Although there are useful military missions that a force of roughly 10,000 U.S. troops can and should perform, it is important to understand that its primary function would be political: Their presence in country would serve as the ultimate guarantee that any Iraqi government would be unable to oppress its people and would reassure all Iraqis that they do not have to fear their security forces, their government, or one another. Especially in current circumstances, with the Hashd ash-Shaabi militias out there and not always responsive to Baghdad's control, such reassurance is critical to Iraq's security and stability. Indeed, this peacekeeping function of U.S. troops is the most important ingredient that was removed from Iraq after 2011. It is a role that scholars have repeatedly identified as critical to preventing the recurrence of civil war.

As part of that, a future American military presence in Iraq needs to be employed to prevent future Iraqi governments from politicizing the Iraqi security forces (ISF) the way that Saddam did and Nuri al-Maliki tried. Here again, Maliki's actions after 2009 are instructive. From 2006 to 2009, the United States painstakingly rebuilt the Iraqi officer corps, identifying good, honest, nationalistic commanders and promoting them, while weeding out the corrupt, the incompetent, and the agents of foreign governments. This effort resulted in an Iraqi military that was not only more capable, but more professional and apolitical. It was a key and underappreciated element of the success of the Surge. It is why predominantly Sunni units of the Iraqi army were welcomed in Basra in the spring of 2008 to eject the Shi'a Jaysh al-Mahdi militia. However, as soon as he had the political space to do so, Maliki went about deliberately reversing that process to ensure that the Iraqi military was wholly subservient to him. He systematically removed the officers the U.S. had appointed, and put in their place those who had been sidelined by the Americans—which ensured their loyalty to him. As a result, by 2012, the Iraqi security forces (ISF) were widely derided as "Maliki's militia." He was able to use them in unconstitutional fashion against his political rivals. To make matters worse, the political hacks Maliki put in charge allowed the ISF to simply stop training, and as a result they lost all cohesion and capability.

American military forces are also needed in Iraq to balance the Iranian (and Lebanese Hizballah) presence that will inevitably persist, along with their allies and proxies among the Hashd ash-Shaabi militias. One of the most important battles Iraq will wage in coming years will be over the status of the Hashid, whether they are properly integrated into the ISF or they become an Iraqi version of the Iranian Revolutionary Guards: a separate military standing apart and reporting to their own masters through a discrete chain of command. The latter would be disastrous, but it cannot be ruled out at this time.

Because of their domestic power and Iranian backing, the Hashid cannot simply be handled by fiat. They need to be slowly assimilated into Iraq's security forces at the individual level. Most of their leaders need to be rewarded for their service to Iraq and given respectable positions within the Iraqi government or else significant pensions for their service. Any attempt to break them or disband them, let alone punish them, could break Iraq instead. But a key will be to build up the power and popularity of the Iraqi government to the point where its leaders can negotiate with the militia leaders (and the Iranians) from a position of much greater leverage. The best way to do that would be to accomplish this will be to take the steps enumerated below to help strengthen the Iraqi government. However, in this area as well, retaining a significant American military presence in country will make it infinitely easier for the Iraqi government to integrate the Hashid into the ISF, and will limit the Hashid's ability to cause mischief (and so cap their political power) if they aren't.

With all of this in mind, Washington should plan to have U.S. troops perform missions in Iraq for at least a decade both to build Iraq's military capabilities and ensure that they are not used against the Iraqi people. A basic list of their specific missions and responsibilities should include:

- U.S. troops need to continue to train the Iraqi military. This means not only those Iraqi brigades that have not yet been retrained by the current U.S. military mission to Iraq, but the entire force repeatedly, in perpetuity. Unfortunately, in the past, whenever the U.S. has ceased to oversee (if not run) the training, the Iraqis have stopped training altogether.

- U.S. advisers should be deployed down to at least army battalion and air force squadron level across the entire ISF, both to help them learn, increase their combat capability, and serve as governors on their behavior. I can remember in 2005 when Iraqi civilians told me that they were always frightened when Iraqi army or police would show up in their towns because they never knew who the soldiers might kill; but they were always reassured if Americans showed up with them, because they knew the Americans would prevent the Iraqi soldiers from causing any harm. Iraq's military has gotten much better since those dark days, but the reassurance function of American forces remains critical as Iraqi society slowly rebuilds trust among its communities.

- U.S. military personnel should continue to assist the Iraqis with tactical intelligence, not only because it will greatly improve its accuracy and utility, but also because it will help the U.S. to monitor developments and prevent internal problems from recurring.

- U.S. military personnel will be necessary to help train the Iraqis with new weaponry, but even more than that to help with the logistics and maintenance of the security forces more broadly. Although in the past the Iraqis were quite adept at logistical operations, since

2003 they have proven utterly hapless (in part because of the computerization of their logistical system by the United States) and without Americans to help, the entire system might grind to a halt.

- It would also be useful to retain some American combat formations in country. The most obvious role they could play would be to assist counterterrorism missions, the need for which is likely to persist for some years to come. More than that, it would be extremely helpful to have American brigades, battalions, and air squadrons rotate into Iraq for lengthy training missions to work with Iraqi forces in realistic exercises, provide the American forces with exposure to the Iraqi operating environment, and serve as an on-hand reserve in the event of foreign aggression or domestic conflict.

Although many of these missions could be performed by relatively small numbers of troops and there is a lot of flexibility in the range I noted above, the number of American troops committed to an enduring, post-ISIS security relationship is very important. The force needs to be big enough to convince Iraqis that the United States remains committed to their security and stability, and committed in ways that it was not after 2011. It is also important because too small a training mission will not be able to maintain (let alone improve) the capabilities of a military as large as the ISF, prevent the re-politicization of the Iraqi military, or monitor developments across most of the country. Such a force would be unlikely to convince any Iraqis that it could keep the peace or strengthen their own military enough so that it could do so itself. That would represent mission failure. It would also create the circumstances for yet another round of civil war.

As a final point regarding a new security cooperation agreement, the U.S. should not get wrapped around the axle about having the Iraqi parliament ratify a Status of Forces Agreement as the Obama Administration did. There are many ways to skin that cat, most entailing far fewer political obstacles, starting with just retaining U.S. forces under the current exchange of letters between Baghdad and Washington from 2014.

Beyond the Security Sector

I am heartened by the fact that it has become a cliché to say that military victory will not be enough to achieve lasting results in Iraq. But I am disheartened that the statement never seems to translate into meaningful U.S. policy. Even the Obama Administration, which so easily could have learned from the mistakes of the Bush 43 Administration, set up 11 "lines of effort" for the Coalition war against ISIS but only fully pursued the two military lines.

This is a shame because Iraq is doing surprisingly well in some areas, even as its basic problems linger ominously in the background. There is still a lot of good material to work with, and some very important positive trends. For instance, most Iraqis want an end to the sectarian violence and are wary of the fearmongering of warlords and militias that led them to civil war twice in the past. Prime Minister Abadi appears to know what has to happen to move Iraq forward and has shown real courage in pursuing it at numerous times in the past, even if his lack of political experience means he sometimes missteps. Moreover, many Iraqis know that the liberation of northern Iraq from Da'ish and the stabilizing of Iraq's economy were only possible because of American assistance and there is a noteworthy consensus among Iraqi leaders (including those most closely tied to Iran) that a residual American military presence and continued American assistance are useful, if not essential.

The Iraqi economy has even shown some modest, positive developments. On my most recent trip to Baghdad in late April 2017, life in the capital had improved noticeably since my previous trip in 2016. The city felt vibrant. There were fewer checkpoints and those I saw appeared to be manned by members of the Iraqi security services, not the Hashd ash-Shaabi as in the past. Billboards thanking Iran for saving Iraq from ISIS were largely gone. The stores appeared to be doing reasonably good business throughout central Baghdad. Goods were flowing in. There were people in the streets and lots of cars on the road. While traffic was bad, it was not crippling. What's more, Iraqis treated it as an inevitable annoyance and rarely let their anger get out of hand. All of this reflects a sense among Iraqis that things are economically okay. Even the usual Iraqi grumbling about shortages seemed diminished—and even when it came to electricity.

The Iraqi oil sector is expanding at a prodigious pace. Production has reached 4.6 million barrels per day (mbd), although Baghdad is keeping its exports below 4 mbd to remain within the current OPEC agreement. By most accounts, the Iraqis plan to keep expanding production to try to reach 5 mbd by the end of the year, although they also insist they will continue to respect any OPEC agreement as long as everyone else does too.

Iraq's financial sector is stable for the moment, but remains problematic and could worsen in the future. The recent financial infusions arranged by the Obama Administration from the World Bank, IMF, and the Coalition, coupled with U.S. loan guarantees have collectively taken the pressure off the Iraqi budget. This has been hugely important. Most civil servants (who represent an excessive percentage of the work force) are getting paid, albeit at lower levels than before 2014. The government is also able to pay key costs for many of its contracts, which has similarly restored salaries for many in the private sector who live off government contracts.

But the loans will prop up Iraq's finances for only a few years. Iraq can't keep borrowing at this rate, and the U.S., IMF, and World Bank shouldn't let it. All need to continue to monitor Iraqi debt carefully to ensure that Iraq doesn't push itself into crisis by overborrowing. Moreover, as a result of corrupt currency exchange policies, Iraq is suffering from a crisis of liquidity. There simply isn't enough money in circulation and the Iraqi central bank is part of the problem, not the solution. As a result, many Iraqis do not have money to purchase anything beyond basic needs, and there is virtually no domestic investment because it is more profitable for the banks to trade currency than to loan money to entrepreneurs. In addition, because of the widespread corruption in the bureaucracy, successful entrepreneurs are systematically fleeced by civil servants unless they have a powerful political figure who can protect them—although in that case, the protector typically robs them to an only slightly lesser degree.

What Iraq Needs from the U.S. Moving Forward
Over the next ten months and the next ten years, where Iraq requires the greatest assistance is in the realm of politics. Iraq's political dysfunctions have been the primary drivers of its internal conflict. They threaten to derail the significant progress made on security matters and the more modest alleviation of Iraq's economic problems. If Iraq cannot get its politics right, then nothing else will matter.

Iraq's political problems can be overcome, but it will be difficult and unlikely that the Iraqis will be able to do it themselves. They need considerable external assistance, principally from the United States, as one of the very few actors with both the capability and the potential willingness to do the right thing for Iraq. That is why the security assistance plan I have outlined above is primarily focused on achieving political goals, not strictly military ones.

Iraq remains badly divided—both in organization and perspective. Its minority Sunni community desperately needs help rebuilding its key towns and cities after their destruction under ISIS. Moreover, they need to see real political reconciliation if they are going to trust Baghdad not to oppress them as the Maliki government did in 2009-2013 (which paved the way for ISIS in the first place). In stark contrast, Iraq's majority Shi'a population is fixated on the need for political, bureaucratic, and economic reform so that they can live the better lives they have been promised since 2003. For their part, Iraq's Kurds are focused on the longer term goal of independence from Iraq and the near-term desire to extract more resources from Baghdad to address their own (even-more-severe) economic problems.

Yet Iraq's political class, particularly its Sunni and Shi'a Arab leaders, are focused on something else entirely: national and provincial elections expected to be held in spring 2018. As a result, most are wholly absorbed with electioneering and political maneuvering and very few actually want to do the hard work of governing—both because it is a distraction and because failure would undermine their election prospects. Consequently, Iraq's communities are all focused on very different goals, all of them difficult to attain on their own, far more so given the lack of unity among them.

There are a welter of other political and politically-inspired problems in Iraq. For instance, the absence of Iraqi security forces has left southern Iraq largely in the hands of tribal militias, organized crime rings, and branches of the Hashd ash-Shaabi militias. This in turn has led to pervasive corruption and growing levels of violence across the south. But all of these other issues, serious as they are, ultimately derive from the core political problems described above. Moreover, they can only be addressed in a meaningful way if Iraq's core political problems are resolved.

The need to help Iraq address these core political problems should therefore guide the formulation of a new, post-ISIS American policy toward Iraq. Moreover, it automatically establishes a set of short and long term goals around which a new American Iraq policy should be organized.

Immediate Priorities

In the near term—the next 6-12 months—the United States should focus on four critical political objectives:

1. Ensuring that Iraq has fair and free elections in spring 2018.

2. Beginning a process of national reconciliation between Sunni and Shi'a to give both a reason to continue negotiations rather than pursue unilateral solutions to their differences.

3. Beginning a process to determine a final, sustainable status for Iraq's Kurdish population.

4. Convincing the Iraqi people that it is possible to reform their corrupt and sclerotic bureaucracy, as well as the wider political system.

After ISIS has been militarily defeated, Iraq's elections are the next critical item on the agenda. They need to be fair and free and that will mean working with the United Nations, our Coalition partners, and the Iraqis themselves to ensure that Iraq's Independent High Election Commission is truly independent—and is seen as such by the Iraqi people and political leadership. Of even greater importance is that the United States cannot make the same mistake it made in 2010. As Emma Sky has so eloquently and passionately explained in her book *The Unraveling*, in those elections, the United States failed to insist that Iraq abide by its own democratic regulations in forming a new government. That failure to stand behind Iraq's rule of law convinced all of Iraq's leaders that the new rules no longer applied and power would instead be apportioned according to Iraq's old rules: corruption, bribery, coercion, and extortion. That is what enabled Nuri al-Maliki to remain as prime minister and freed him to act in ever more extra-constitutional or unconstitutional fashion.

At virtually the same time, Iraq's Sunni populace needs to be reintegrated into its political system, its administrative apparatus, and its economy. It was Maliki's alienation of that Sunni community—his arrest of so many of its political leaders, his exclusion of a great many Iraqis from jobs in the government and security services, his deprivation of Sunni provinces of funding and government services—that drove them into the arms of ISIS in the first place. Preventing a recurrence of civil war will mean doing the opposite, or at least getting started to the extent possible, to give Sunnis a reason to remain patient and not take other precipitous action. Consequently, in the short term, until a wider national reconciliation and political restructuring can take place, that is likely to mean apportioning ministries and other key positions to Sunni leaders, integrating more Sunnis into the security services, designating various public sector jobs for Sunnis, allocating funds via provincial governments for reconstruction, and initiating government contracts (particularly infrastructure development) in predominantly Sunni areas of the country.

Beyond this, it is critical to the interests of both the Iraqi and American governments that Baghdad be seen as addressing the most pressing needs of all of its people and doing so in the next 6-12 months, preferably before the Iraqi elections. That does not mean that Baghdad needs to fix every problem. Just that they need to be seen as *trying* to fix the most important ones. The best way to do that would be for the U.S. and Iraqi governments to identify a handful of important, high-profile projects that can show tangible progress in a year or less and that would have a meaningful impact on Iraqi lives.

To their credit, some within the Iraqi government are thinking in smart and creative ways about how to make such moves. Prime Minister Abadi has made this a priority, and the economic reform planning team in his office is looking at further subsidy cuts, pro-growth policies, and anti-corruption measures including the introduction of extensive "e-government" practices that would improve efficiency. The Ministry of Planning is pushing forward a scheme to build several major roads, including a new super highway from Baghdad to Amman, Jordan that would include tributary roads to connect the many towns of Anbar province, and financing for business development to turn the entire network into a major economic pathway, something like an Iraqi "Route 66." (This would also be a great example of a government infrastructure project in the Sunni areas.)

Other Iraqi technocrats are pushing for a major overhaul and upgrade of the banking system, to shut down the corrupt currency exchange practices, create an electronic banking system, and push cash back into the economy to revive both consumption and investment. Some Iraqi expatriates have argued for an international effort to build hospitals and health clinics across Iraq. Iraq's healthcare sector has been decimated by the wars and sanctions and it would make a major and immediate impact on people's lives if they had access to better quality healthcare. However, all of these plans remain in their infancy and all will be major lifts for Iraq's weak bureaucracy and paralyzed political system. Given Baghdad's record over the past

14 years, no one should bet heavily that any of them will come to fruition without major assistance from the international community.

Broader Goals of a New U.S. Policy Toward Iraq
Over the longer term, the United States needs to invest its resources and energy into three related but overarching issues:

1. Mediating a national reconciliation process among senior Iraqi leaders (primarily Sunni and Shi'a);

2. Helping to reform the Iraqi bureaucratic and political systems to improve the effectiveness of Iraqi governance and enable a decentralization of authority and resources from Baghdad to the provinces;

3. And overseeing talks between Baghdad and Erbil over the status of Iraqi Kurdistan.

National Reconciliation, Power-Sharing, and Decentralization. Iraq's communities have (once again) lost their trust in one another. Trust is always the first casualty of civil war, and Iraq had only started to rebuild it in 2007-2009 before the American withdrawal allowed Maliki to pursue a sectarian agenda and destroy Sunni trust of the Shi'a all over again. Now and for the foreseeable future, rebuilding that trust must be a top priority.

In part for that reason, Iraq will almost certainly need to transition (eventually) to a combination of federalism and either confederation with the Kurds or, more likely, eventual independence for an Iraqi Kurdish state.

As with the short term, so over the long term, the United States needs to take on board the difficult task of helping the Iraqis forge a new national reconciliation agreement, either formally or informally. There is simply no way around this foundational requirement. Iraqis need a new power-sharing agreement that will allow all of the rival communities, but particularly the Sunni and Shi'a Arabs, to begin cooperating again. Without this, the military successes against ISIS will evaporate.

In recent months, both the United States and the government of Iraq have trumpeted local reconciliation efforts as a bottom-up substitute for a top-down process of national reconciliation. While such grass-roots efforts can be very useful, historically they are no substitute for high-level reconciliation. Without the latter, local efforts are typically undone by rivalries among senior leaders and the result, once again, is renewed civil war. Yet the United States has made far too little effort to bring Iraq's senior leadership together, hiding behind Baghdad's desire to handle this itself and the self-fulfilling prophecy that Iraq's leaders are too fragmented. The current, Iraqi-led "process" has so far achieved nothing. On the other hand, it is worth noting that in 2007-2008, my friend and co-panelist today, Ambassador Ryan Crocker, faced a similar problem of fragmented leadership, yet he and his team brokered exactly the kind of (informal but effective) national reconciliation that Iraq desperately needs once again

As part of such an agreement—and because the opposite approach had failed miserably by 2014, paving the way for ISIS—Iraq will have to develop a federal structure (as envisioned in the current Iraqi constitution) that delegates greater authority and autonomy to its various ethnic, sectarian and geographic components. The traumatic experiences of three and a half decades of Saddam's tyranny, two bouts of civil war, and Maliki's brutal attempt to consolidate power in between, have made it inconceivable that Iraq's communities will accept a return to an all-powerful, highly-centralized Iraqi state.

However, in fittingly ironic fashion, the goal of a more decentralized, federal political system now requires a dedicated effort to *strengthen* Iraq's central government. The problem is best understood this way: Decentralization can take two forms, empowerment or entropy. Obviously, the latter is a positive that can produce a functional state, the latter a disaster likely to produce war and misery. Decentralization via empowerment requires a reasonably strong and functional central government that grants specific authorities and the power to execute those tasks to subordinate and/or peripheral entities. Decentralization via entropy, in contrast, occurs when the central government lacks the strength to control its constituent parts—let alone to empower them—and so subordinates, peripheral entities, and actors outside the system altogether simply grab authority and resources and do with it whatever they like. Not only does such anarchy invariably dissolve into chaos and conflict, but the actors arrogating power to themselves are rarely as strong as they would be if their power were delegated by an effective central government. One example of the distinction is the United States created by the Articles of Confederation compared to the United States created by the U.S. Constitution. Under the former, the central government was too weak and so the federal structure did not work, even though the states were far more powerful than they were under the Constitution. The result was anarchy, chaos and internal conflict. The Constitution provided for a stronger central government, which paradoxically made a stable federal system—with still strong states—both practical and functional.

Unfortunately, what has been happening in Iraq for the past several years is largely decentralization by entropy, not empowerment, and that is another factor that could produce renewed conflict in the future. It is this entropic pull that is causing the fragmentation that is now the leitmotif of Iraqi politics. The Sunnis have long suffered from a badly atomized leadership, but even that has worsened in recent years, exacerbated by Maliki's brilliance in targeting any moderate, capable and charismatic Sunni leader who might have unified that community. Yet the Shi'a leadership is also fracturing. Iraqis often like to argue that the Marja'iye (the Shi'a religious establishment centered in Najaf) provides the Shi'a with a unified voice, but if that were ever true, it is proving less and less so. Now, dozens of Shi'a figures can claim leadership over important constituencies, including dozens of new militias, many of which operate outside the control of the central government. This centrifugal trajectory simultaneously paralyzes the Iraqi political system and pushes the country toward chaos and renewed conflict.

The Kurdish Question. Although I am certainly open to the prospect of a Kurdish-Iraqi federation or confederation if the Kurds truly want it, I strongly suspect that Kurdish secession is the only real solution to the problem. The Kurds constitute a separate nation who have made clear for the past century that they do not want to be a part of Arab Iraq. Their forced inclusion in the Iraqi state has resulted in nothing but conflict and misery for *both* the Kurds and the Arabs. I say that as someone who considers himself a friend to both, and believes that Kurdish secession would benefit both peoples. As I noted earlier, Kurdistan is a liability to Iraq, not an asset.

If Iraq and the Kurds would both be better off with an amicable divorce, ensuring that such a separation does not provoke a war of its own is going to be a challenge. The Kurds and Iraqis have a great deal to hash out and both sides have conflicting claims and passionate attachments to their own positions. Likewise, as we have seen in the latest drama over last week's Kurdish referendum, the Iranians are likely to oppose Kurdish secession, and the Turks and Sunni Arab states may do so as well.

Thus, ensuring the amicability of a Kurdish-Iraqi divorce will take time, goodwill and constructive diplomacy that seem in short supply right now. The United States has important interests in seeing this separation happen peacefully, but little else. How the Kurds and Arabs will choose to define their borders, handle territorial issues (including the status of Kirkuk and the distribution of oilfields), and decide the fate of displaced persons are not issues on which the United States needs to take a position. However, it will be critical that Washington serve as honest broker in helping the parties find solutions that both can accept. It may also be necessary for the United States to help each side make painful concessions, in part by providing bilateral or multilateral aid as compensation. Allowing the Kurds to opt out of Iraq would also increase the demographic (and therefore electoral) weight of Iraq's Shi'a Arab community, which will make it all the more important for the United States to help Arab Iraq devise a more stable, equitable and self-regulating political system of its own.

The Obama Administration put considerable effort into handling the pressing troubles between Baghdad and Erbil, and this helped achieve a certain political stability and some remarkable military cooperation. However, without the framework of a long-term plan that creates the circumstances for peaceful Kurdish secession (along the lines of the Czechoslovak model) these near-term gains will erode and eventually collapse as they have so regularly in the past.

Consequently, the United States should inaugurate Iraqi-Kurdish talks on two parallel, simultaneous tracks: One focusing on a long-term process for eventual, peaceful Kurdish secession, and a second focusing on Baghdad-Erbil relations in the short term, to include sticky issues like security cooperation, administration of Kurdish occupied territory, oil revenues, and fiscal policy. The latter might produce an agreement on a new federal or confederal structure by which Kurdistan would remain part of Iraq until the longer-term process produced a workable solution that all sides could accept.

Leverage

None of this can happen if the United States doesn't preserve and continuously rebuild its leverage with Iraq. Many Iraqis and some foreign governments will oppose aspects of the short and long-term agendas outlined above and the United States will have to be able to push back on them directly or empower Iraqis to do so. Similarly, few Iraqis will embrace the tasks that are needed to build a better Iraq—and secure America's interests by doing so—if they are not given the help they need and the tools they lack.

Part of preserving America's influence in Iraq comes from preserving a robust American military presence there. There is no better way to "empower" the Iraqis we seek to aid than by protecting them, creating a peaceful environment in which they can work, and giving them the strength to take on the bad actors who seek to employ violence, ignore the rule of law, and otherwise work outside Iraq's democratic system. Other Iraqis will benefit from that presence in a variety of ways, from securing contracts with the U.S. to enjoying the security created by that presence. Indeed, many bad actors will *lose* influence as a result of that presence since it will be harder for them to use force as an element of their own leverage.

Economic assistance would be a superb adjunct to an ongoing American security commitment. As I noted above, the bilateral and international financial assistance arranged for Iraq by the Obama Administration have been very helpful in stabilizing Iraq's finances in the short term, but they are not a long-term solution. Additional foreign aid could also have an outsized effect in Iraq because Baghdad is so inefficient, corrupt and bottlenecked that external assistance provided directly to those who will spend it comes faster and is of greater utility than trying to squeeze dinars through the Iraqi political process.

Moreover, as with a 10,000-man military commitment, an economic aid program of (ideally) $1-2 billion per year for five years would reinforce to Iraqis that the United States is making a long-term commitment to Iraq's stability and development. Symbolically, that is worth far more than the practical impact of the dollars spent. It is also the case that, if that money is spent wisely, it can be used to empower moderate Iraqi leaders looking to move past sectarian differences and break the deadlocks suffocating the Iraqi political system.

Beyond the possibility of American economic assistance looms the tantalizing prospect of GCC aid. Obviously, Kuwait, Qatar, the UAE, and conceivably Saudi Arabia could provide even greater economic support to Iraq, and do so more easily than the United States. The recent moves by the Saudis to dramatically expand their ties with Iraq are therefore an extremely hopeful development. Riyadh appears to have finally recognized that Iraq is not lost to Iran, and is now trying to ensure that it does not become another Iranian dominion. GCC economic aid guided by American know-how and secured by an American military presence would be an ideal way of providing Iraq with the resources it needs to succeed. Consequently, U.S. policy to Iraq should continue to push for GCC economic assistance to Iraq.

The Iranian Dimension

Although American influence in Baghdad has grown significantly over the past two years, Iran is still the most important foreign power in Iraq. We may not like it, but the reality is that the United States is unlikely to accomplish much there if Tehran is determined to thwart us. It would require a massive commitment of American resources to Iraq to allow Washington to replace Tehran as the most influential external player in Baghdad.

However, Iran has always demonstrated that it has a hierarchy of interests in Iraq and is nothing if not ruthlessly pragmatic. Without going into a long explanation of Iranian motives in Iraq and the evidence for them, what is most important is that Iran has not tried to stop the United States from doing what it has been doing in Iraq since 2014. Moreover, on several occasions Iran has provided critical, if tacit, assistance for those efforts. What Tehran appears to see as its principle interest in Iraq is having a unified Iraq under a democratic government— which is the best assurance that Iraq will be both stable and dominated by its Shi'a community, which will always want to be on decent terms with Tehran.

Although significant differences over Iraq could arise in future between the U.S. and Iran, especially over the role of the Hashd ash-Shaabi, there is nothing about the steps I have outlined above that runs contrary to Iran's core interests in Iraq, and much that is entirely consistent with them. It would even be useful for the United States to see if some degree of coordination out of shared interests may be possible. That would be especially helpful to try to secure Iranian buy-in for longer term American objectives such as a greater political role for the Sunni Arab community and eventual independence for Iraq's Kurds, both of which Iran opposes at present.

Moreover, influential as it is, Iran is not all-powerful in Iraq and has not been since the Battle of Qadisiyah in 637 AD. Left to their own devices, most Iraqis would shut out the Iranians altogether, and they have done so whenever they were strong enough, despite all of Iran's levers for wielding influence in Iraq. That then is the key for those seeking to diminish or eliminate Iranian influence in Iraq: building a strong, cohesive Iraq that has the confidence to show the Iranians the door. And that, of course, is precisely the goal of the approach I have outlined above.

Doing the Right Thing. . . Finally

President Obama liked to intone that Americans cannot do what Iraqis need to do for themselves. At best, that statement was a tautology and therefore useless as a guide to policy. In truth, it was merely an incorrect excuse for American inactivity. Time and again since the 2003 invasion, we have seen that the Iraqis cannot do the most important things that they need to do on their own, but have been able to do them with American help.

It is equally wrong to believe, as many in the previous Administration once claimed, that American assistance allowed the Iraqis to indulge their worst habits and avoid taking the hard steps they needed to for the good of their country. These same officials insisted that removing the United States from the equation would force the Iraqis to finally do the right thing because they had no other choice. In reality, whenever the Iraqis have found themselves in such circumstances, they invariably have made the worst choice, to their detriment and ours.

They do so not necessarily because they are knaves or fools (although some undoubtedly are). They do so because they are caught in a Hobbesian state of nature, the war of all against all, in which self-preservation argues for taking actions that marginally improve one's own position at the expense of everyone else's. That, in turn, forces everyone else to do the same and so renders everyone less and less safe and secure. It is the common path to civil war.

Escaping such circumstances typically requires an external actor capable of creating better, more cooperative outcomes for everyone. That is the role the United States successfully played during the Surge of 2007-2008 and also at times since 2014. It is a role we must continue to play in the future if we are to prevent Iraq sliding back into the civil war trap.

I am very fond of Winston Churchill's famous quip that, "You can always count on Americans to do the right thing—after they've tried everything else." In Iraq, haven't we tried everything else? Isn't it finally time to do the right thing?

Kenneth Pollack
Resident Scholar

Middle East political-military affairs (with an emphasis on Iraq, Iran, Syria, and Saudi Arabia)
US-Middle East security and foreign policies

Kenneth M. Pollack is a resident scholar at the American Enterprise Institute (AEI), where he works on Middle Eastern political-military affairs, focusing in particular on Iran, Iraq, Saudi Arabia, and the Gulf countries.

Before joining AEI, Dr. Pollack was affiliated with the Brookings Institution, where he was a senior fellow at the Saban Center for Middle East Policy. Before that, he was the center's director and director of research. Dr. Pollack served twice at the National Security Council, first as director for Near East and South Asian affairs and then as director for Persian Gulf affairs. He began his career as a Persian Gulf military analyst at the CIA, where he was the principal author of the CIA's classified postmortem on Iraqi strategy and military operations during the Persian Gulf War. Among other recognitions, Dr. Pollack was awarded the CIA's Exceptional Performance Award twice and the Certificate of Distinction for Outstanding Performance of Duty, both for work on the Persian Gulf War.

Dr. Pollack has also worked on long-term issues related to Middle Eastern political and military affairs for the Joint Chiefs of Staff when he was a senior research professor at the Institute for National Security Studies at National Defense University.

Dr. Pollack is the author of nine books, including "Unthinkable: Iran, the Bomb, and American Strategy" (Simon & Schuster, 2013), named one of the "Best Books of 2013" by The Economist and one of the "100 Notable Books of 2013" by The New York Times; "A Path out of the Desert: A Grand Strategy for America in the Middle East" (Random House, 2008), a Washington Post and Foreign Affairs bestseller, which was chosen as one of The Washington Post's "Best Books of the Year" for 2008 and as an editor's choice of The New York Times Book Review; "The Persian Puzzle: The Conflict Between Iran and America" (Random House, 2004); and "The Threatening Storm: The Case for Invading Iraq" (Random House, 2002), a New York Times and Washington Post bestseller.

Dr. Pollack is the author of numerous articles and has been published in The Washington Post, Foreign Affairs, and The Atlantic, among others.

He received his bachelor's from Yale University and a doctorate in political science from the Massachusetts Institute of Technology.

DISCLOSURE FORM FOR WITNESSES
COMMITTEE ON ARMED SERVICES
U.S. HOUSE OF REPRESENTATIVES

INSTRUCTION TO WITNESSES: Rule 11, clause 2(g)(5), of the Rules of the U.S. House of Representatives for the 115th Congress requires nongovernmental witnesses appearing before House committees to include in their written statements a curriculum vitae and a disclosure of the amount and source of any federal contracts or grants (including subcontracts and subgrants), or contracts or payments originating with a foreign government, received during the current and two previous calendar years either by the witness or by an entity represented by the witness and related to the subject matter of the hearing. This form is intended to assist witnesses appearing before the House Committee on Armed Services in complying with the House rule. Please note that a copy of these statements, with appropriate redactions to protect the witness's personal privacy (including home address and phone number) will be made publicly available in electronic form not later than one day after the witness's appearance before the committee. Witnesses may list additional grants, contracts, or payments on additional sheets, if necessary.

Witness name: Kenneth M. Pollack

Capacity in which appearing: (check one)

☐ Individual

☒ Representative

If appearing in a representative capacity, name of the company, association or other entity being represented: American Enterprise Institute

Federal Contract or Grant Information: If you or the entity you represent before the Committee on Armed Services has contracts (including subcontracts) or grants (including subgrants) with the federal government, please provide the following information:

2017

Federal grant/ contract	Federal agency	Dollar value	Subject of contract or grant
n/a			

2016

Foreign contract/ payment	Foreign government	Dollar value	Subject of contract or payment
n/a			

2015

Foreign contract/ payment	Foreign government	Dollar value	Subject of contract or payment
n/a			

Securing the Peace after the Fall of ISIS
Testimony Prepared for House Armed Services Committee, Subcommittee on Oversight and Investigations
Dr. Marc Lynch, Professor of Political Science at The George Washington University and Nonresident Senior Associate, Carnegie Endowment for International Peace Middle East Program
27 September 2017

Thank you, Chairman Thornberry and Ranking Member Smith of the House Armed Services Committee, and Chairman Hartzler and Ranking Member Moulton of this Subcommittee, for this invitation to speak about the critically important question of Iraqi stability after the fall of ISIS. The U.S.-led coalition has made impressive progress over the last three years towards containing, degrading, and ultimately defeating the Islamic State in Iraq. It is heartening that this committee is paying serious attention to what comes next. Nothing could be more important in order to consolidate these successes and avoid yet another recurrence of insurgency and state failure in Iraq. Representative Moulton has led the way on this with his presentation last year of a "Plan to Secure the Peace in Iraq."[1]

The campaign against ISIS has benefited from impressive bipartisan support. The Trump administration wisely chose to continue the strategy against the Islamic State designed by the Obama administration. The Global Coalition against ISIS has effectively coordinated a broad international and regional group, while the CJTF of Operation Iraqi Resolve has executed an effective military strategy of building and supporting the Iraqi Security Force. The campaign stopped the Islamic State's advance, and then systematically closed off its borders, degraded its capabilities and steadily recaptured its territory. Critically, it worked to create both Iraqi and regional political support for the campaign, paying careful attention to the urgent needs of civilians in the areas liberated from ISIS and worked closely with a wide range of international NGOs to assist the displaced. The pace of military advances has accelerated since the liberation of Mosul in July and of Tel Afar last week. It is likely that in the relatively near future the remaining ISIS strongholds in Iraq will be recaptured. The accelerated pace of the campaign in turn increases the urgency of addressing numerous looming challenges to stability and peace in a post-ISIS Iraq.

There is a near consensus among analysts that military victory against ISIS must be followed by a political and economic reconstruction strategy in order to prevent another resurgence of insurgency or Iraqi state failure.[2] The U.S. should assume that

---

[1] Rep. Seth Moulton, "A Plan to Secure the Peace in Iraq," 13 September 2016.
[2] Several major recent reports make this point. For examples, see Shelly Culbertson and Linda Robinson, *Making Victory Count After Defeating ISIS* (Washington, DC: RAND Corporation, 2017); International Crisis Group, *Counter-terrorism Pitfalls: What the U.S. Fight Against ISIS and al-Qaeda Should Avoid* (Special Report #3, 22 March 2017); Amb. Ryan Crocker, *Report of the Task Force on the Future of Iraq* (Washington, D.C.: Atlantic Council, 31 May 2017).

after its territorial defeat, ISIS will attempt to re-embed, regroup, and continue a violent insurgent campaign at a lower level.[3] If the defeat of ISIS leads to another round of Shi'ite sectarian governance, unmet promises of political accommodation to the Iraqi Sunni community, and reconstruction aid siphoned off into corruption, then this insurgency is more likely to gain traction and the Iraqi state is likely to prove far less resilient.

The military success against ISIS has created a political opening to strike a new political compact. In an April 2017 survey carried out by the leading Iraqi polling organization IIACSS and just published in the *Washington Post*, 51% of Sunnis say Iraq going in right direction and 71% of Sunnis say they support Prime Minister Al-Abadi.[4] This is a far cry from the alienation reported in the summer 2014 survey, carried out just before ISIS swept through Mosul, in which only 5% of Sunnis said they supported then Prime Minister Maliki. But this optimism is fragile: in the IIACSS survey, 61% of Sunnis fear ISIS could return to liberated areas. There are rampant reports of sectarian abuses against Sunnis in these areas and of shortcomings in reconstruction and governance. Furthermore, the Sunni political class has been decimated, the Shi'ite political landscape is fragmented, and there are widespread indicators of youth alienation from the political process.[5]

There are innumerable issues confronting the Iraqi state in the coming months and years. In addition to the immediate crisis over the future of the KRG within Iraq, I would like to highlight three other issues critical to the post-ISIS period: institutionalizing relations between the U.S. and Iraq in a conditional partnership; helping to anticipate and address persistent failures in governance and state capacity, particularly given the possibility of reduced presence by international humanitarian organizations; and balancing competition and cooperation with Iran in the Iraqi theater.

(1) Managing the Kurdish Referendum Fallout: While Iraq's Kurds have a powerful case and strong internal support for national independence, the independence referendum held on September 25, 2017, risks significantly disrupting the anti-ISIS campaign and the stability of the Iraqi political system. The United States was correct to oppose the referendum on strategic grounds, but at this point the imperative must be to mitigate its impact on Iraqi stability. Politicians in Baghdad have been engaging in highly inflammatory rhetoric and escalatory actions which could spin out of control. Regional actors such as Turkey have also inflamed

---

[3] Michael Knights, "Predicting the Shape of Iraq's Next Sunni Insurgency," *CTC Sentinel* (August 2017).

[4] Munqith Dagher and Karl Kaltenthaler, "Iraqi Sunnis Are Impressed by the Defeat of ISIS. Here's What That Could Mean." *Washington Post (Monkey Cage)*, 11 September 2017.

[5] On the importance of Iraqi youth alienation, see the report by the International Crisis Group, *Fight or Flight: The Desperate Plight of Iraq's Generation 2000* (Middle East Report 169, 6 August 2016).

the situation with military and political threats. Calming down the situation and laying foundations for a longer-term political process now must be a top priority.

U.S. efforts to leverage its strong military and political relationship with the Iraqi Kurdish leadership, including unusually public U.S. warnings, against holding the referendum failed to prevent it. Rather than retaliate, at this point the U.S. should focus on managing the fallout. It should urge Kurdish leaders to avoid provocative moves in the aftermath of the referendum, to engage directly with Baghdad on future steps, and to remain focused on the need to finish the campaign against ISIS. At the regional level, the U.S. should urge neighbors such as Turkey to restrain from military threats and show restraint, and to scale back threatened economic boycotts and air travel bans. The U.S. should also engage with Iraqi politicians across the political and identity spectrum to calm the sharply spiking anti-Kurdish politics, urging the Iraqi Parliament and government to avoid the extreme forms of retaliation which are currently being publicly discussed.

(2) Conditional Partnership: Looking beyond the immediate crisis, the United States should make clear its commitment to supporting a durable and sustainable post-ISIS Iraq. This commitment should not be open-ended, however. It should be defined through a conditional partnership which reinforces positive trends without enabling destructive possible paths. Such a conditional partnership, cemented in a mutually agreeable Memorandum of Understanding and Status of Forces Agreement, should allow the U.S. to constructively support the Iraqi government without being drawn ever deeper into unsustainable military commitments.

This partnership should be based on clear expectations about political reforms. Such political reform is inextricably linked with enduring security. A primary driver of the return of the Islamic State as a potent insurgency after 2012 was the opening created by former Prime Minister Nuri al-Maliki's sectarian and failed governance. Both before and after the U.S. withdrawal, Maliki consistently resisted U.S. pressure to incorporate Awakening and Sons of Iraq fighters into the security forces and the implementation of agreements towards political accommodation.

The situation today is more conducive to an effective, conditional partnership. The U.S. military returned to Iraq at the invitation of the Iraqi government to meet a common threat, and its strategy is designed to support the Iraqi military rather than taking the lead role. This has reduced the salience of anti-American sentiment, offering greater freedom of political maneuver for defining the U.S.-Iraqi relationship. After the bitter experience of 2014, Iraqi political leaders today can have few illusions about the costs of losing American military and political support.

Prime Minister al-Abadi has proven more sympathetic to the needs for political reforms, despite his relatively weak position and the significant challenges from competing Shi'ite parties and movements. Victory over ISIS has given Abadi a significant if fleeting political boost, and the opportunity to take a stronger position within Iraq's fragmented political system. This will not last long, however. Political rivals such as former Prime Minister Maliki have been exploiting the Kurdish referendum and other contentious political issues to undermine Abadi. The U.S. should reward Abadi's partnership with a commitment to a long-term, institutionalized relationship which allows him to translate success against ISIS into more enduring reforms. Conditioning future military support on clear political expectations will give the U.S. greater leverage, while allowing it to remain actively engaged in Iraq without either endlessly expanding military commitments or unconditional support to a corrupt and unaccountable political elite.

U.S. expectations and contributions should include continued support for building state capacity in vital sectors. Security sector reform remains essential, including rebuilding Iraq's depleted elite counter-terrorism forces and reorienting training of conventional forces to deal with a low-level insurgency in ways that do not alienate local populations.[6] The U.S. should also help find a path for properly integrating, and professionalizing portions of the Shi'ite PMF (Hashd) within the structures of the Iraqi state, to avoid a replay of the costly failure to manage the Sunni Awakenings and "Sons of Iraq" after the Surge. The PMF represent a variety of political and institutional interests and should not be treated as a monolithic grouping of pro-Iranian militias. Some PMF units provided essential manpower in the early days of the campaign against ISIS when the Iraqi Security Forces were in disarray, and continued to play a role in subsequent campaigns. Indeed, their future has become a key dimension of intense intra-Shi'a political battles which should be carefully followed. The U.S. should support efforts to integrate those PMF units willing to be included within a unified and nonsectarian state, while supporting state efforts to disarm and demobilize those aligned with hardline sectarian forces.[7]

The priority of political accord should inform the execution of the final stages of the anti-ISIS military campaign. The careful attention to civilian casualties, careful pace of military advance, and preparation for post-liberation security and assistance over the first few years of the campaign were key to the building of popular support. The rising civilian casualties in recent months are driven by multiple factors: an intensifying air campaign, ISIS strategy of preventing civilian flight, the nature of urban combat in populated areas. Whatever the cause, these well-publicized civilian casualties risk undermining the political support which has been so essential to the long-term durability of the campaign and feed support for a revived insurgency. The U.S. should redouble its efforts to sustain a cautious and patient approach designed to minimize civilian casualties and to deny effective propaganda to future insurgents.

(3) Governance and State Capacity: Weak state capacity and failed governance has long been at the root of many of Iraq's problems. The inability of the state to

---

[6] On the degradation of the elite counterterrorism forces, see Kirk Sowell, "Mosul and the Limits of State Capacity," *Sada* (Carnegie Endowment for International Peace, 30 March 2017).

[7] Renad Mansour and Faleh Jabar, *The Popular Mobilization Forces and Iraq's Future* (Carnegie Middle East Center, April 2017)

provide security, services or accountable government feeds public alienation and undermines economic recovery. Pockets of state failure strike particularly hard in Sunni-majority areas, rural areas, and in communities with large numbers of Internally Displaced Persons. Persistent electricity shortages, water problems, and inadequate services have driven popular protests. Budget shortfalls, administrative incapacity, rampant corruption, and ongoing violence and displacement have impeded even well-intended efforts to improve state services.

The shortcomings of the Iraqi state have proven resistant to external solutions. Corruption, sectarianism, and ineffective bureaucracies erode the state from within, and undermine state legitimacy. In a 2013 survey carried out by the highly respected Arab Barometer, 88.3% of Iraqis agreed that there is corruption in state institutions. This complicates international efforts to build state capacity, since external money for reconstruction risks being lost into a vast pit of corruption or misdirected for the purposes of political patronage. Even without such corruption challenges, Iraqi oil production is barely sufficient to cover government operating costs, much less to finance reconstruction.[8]

The very urgency of the challenges has provided a strong incentive for the Iraqi state to work effectively with their international counterparts. The anti-ISIS coalition has done an impressive job coordinating the humanitarian response with international non governmental organizations. Nearly 150 international NGOs have supported civilians displaced from Mosul and other areas liberated from ISIS, but the needs remain overwhelming.[9] The Office for Coordinating Humanitarian Affairs in Iraq estimates that there currently 3.4 million displaced overall, with more than 11 million Iraqis in need of assistance.[10]

The very success of the international humanitarian response creates another potential risk, however. Their high level of commitment has alleviated the burden on the Iraqi state. But the high level of international assistance could easily dry up as international attention and funding moves on to other crisis areas. This could be fatal for post-ISIS Iraq, if these areas experience a precipitous decline in essential services following liberation. The United States and the Global Coalition must work to ensure continuity in services, so that such a vacuum does not appear and that Iraqis in liberated areas experience improved lives rather than abandonment and heightened misery. These services must be connected directly and visibly to the Iraqi state, not only to NGOs, in order to help build the legitimacy and accountability of local and national government.

The focus on state capacity and governance should emphasize the importance of decentralization and local autonomy. Prime Minister al-Abadi has been receptive to

---

[8] A recent evaluation of Iraq's oil production found systematic shortfalls in its ability to cover regular government operating expenses, with no surplus for capital investment. See *Inside Iraqi Politics* 159 (21 July 2017), p.8.
[9] IOM-Iraq Sitrep #30, 10-23 August 2017.
[10] Most recent figures from OCHA-Iraq Humanitarian Dashboard (July 2017)

such moves, which command significant support across the Iraqi political spectrum and the international community alike. Drafting a new provincial elections law has proven challenging, however, and the elections have been postponed until 2018.[11] Such a focus on local governance could help to meet the urgent demands of youth protestors who complain of persistent unaccountability and dysfunction of the central state, and could also facilitate more systematic addressing of the needs of the internally displaced.

(4) Finding the Right Balance With Iran: Iraq's relationship with Iran should not be allowed to become a fatal obstacle to the anti-ISIS campaign or the long-term relationship with Iraq. Given the urgency of the threat posed by ISIS after the fall of Mosul, the U.S. wisely chose to prioritize the battle against ISIS over competition with Iran in the Iraqi theater. Forcing the government of Iraq to choose between Iran and the United States would have guaranteed failure in the campaign against ISIS. It would be natural for the Iranian-US tacit cooperation to fray as the IS threat diminishes, but this would be a critical mistake which would undermine all which has been so patiently achieved. The commitment to prioritizing the fight against ISIS should extend to the post-ISIS struggle to support a sustainable Iraqi political accord. The potential for deterioration of relations with Iran over the JCPOA is beyond the scope of this testimony, but must not be allowed to spill over into Iraq.

More broadly, the United States should contest Iranian influence in Iraq, but it can not end it. A sharp deterioration of relations with Iran, whether over compliance with the Joint Comprehensive Plan of Agreement or over its proxies in Iraq, would have devastating and rapid effects on the anti-ISIL campaign. The U.S. must therefore continue to seek an appropriate balance between contesting Iranian influence in Iraq and working with Iranian-backed forces towards a common interest in defeating ISIS and sustaining a stable Iraq. The restoration of Saudi presence in Iraq could be a positive, as long as it contributes to the rebuilding of the Sunni community as part of a shared political project and not towards harnessing them to a destructive confrontation with Iranian-backed groups in Iraq.

In conclusion, the campaign against the Islamic State in Iraq has produced significant positive results, with bipartisan support. A comprehensive approach to partnership with Iraq should now prioritize institutionalizing that relationship, protecting Iraqis in newly liberated areas, encouraging political reforms, building state capacity, and sustaining international humanitarian assistance. These steps will be essential to building the resilience of the Iraqi state in the face of the Islamic State's likely return to new forms of insurgency following the collapse of its state.

---

[11] Kirk Sowell, "Wrangling over Iraq's Election Laws," *Sada* (Carnegie Endowment for International Peace, 20 April 2017).

Marc Lynch

Marc Lynch is professor of political science at The George Washington University, where he served as director of the Institute for Middle East Studies from 2009-2015. He is the founder and director of the Project on Middle East Political Science, a Nonresident Senior Associate at the Carnegie Endowment for International Peace Middle East Program, and a 2016 Andrew Carnegie Fellow. He is also a contributing editor to the Washington Post's Monkey Cage political science page. His most recent book, The New Arab Wars: Anarchy and Uprising in the Middle East, was published last year by Public Affairs.

DISCLOSURE FORM FOR WITNESSES
COMMITTEE ON ARMED SERVICES
U.S. HOUSE OF REPRESENTATIVES

INSTRUCTION TO WITNESSES: Rule 11, clause 2(g)(5), of the Rules of the U.S. House of Representatives for the 115th Congress requires nongovernmental witnesses appearing before House committees to include in their written statements a curriculum vitae and a disclosure of the amount and source of any federal contracts or grants (including subcontracts and subgrants), or contracts or payments originating with a foreign government, received during the current and two previous calendar years either by the witness or by an entity represented by the witness and related to the subject matter of the hearing. This form is intended to assist witnesses appearing before the House Committee on Armed Services in complying with the House rule. Please note that a copy of these statements, with appropriate redactions to protect the witness's personal privacy (including home address and phone number) will be made publicly available in electronic form not later than one day after the witness's appearance before the committee. Witnesses may list additional grants, contracts, or payments on additional sheets, if necessary.

Witness name: Marc Lynch

Capacity in which appearing: (check one)

☒ Individual

☐ Representative

If appearing in a representative capacity, name of the company, association or other entity being represented: ____

Federal Contract or Grant Information: If you or the entity you represent before the Committee on Armed Services has contracts (including subcontracts) or grants (including subgrants) with the federal government, please provide the following information:

2017

Federal grant/ contract	Federal agency	Dollar value	Subject of contract or grant
N/A			

2016

Federal grant/ contract	Federal agency	Dollar value	Subject of contract or grant
N/A			

2015

Federal grant/ contract	Federal agency	Dollar value	Subject of contract or grant
N/A			

<u>Foreign Government Contract or Payment Information</u>: If you or the entity you represent before the Committee on Armed Services has contracts or payments originating from a foreign government, please provide the following information:

2017

Foreign contract/ payment	Foreign government	Dollar value	Subject of contract or payment
N/A			

2016

Foreign contract/ payment	Foreign government	Dollar value	Subject of contract or payment
N/A			

2015

Foreign contract/ payment	Foreign government	Dollar value	Subject of contract or payment
N/A			

WRITTEN TESTIMONY ON "SECURING THE PEACE AFTER THE FALL OF ISIL"
HOUSE ARMED SERVICES COMMITTEE
SUBCOMMITTEE ON OVERSIGHT AND INVESTIGATIONS
Tuesday, October 3, 2017

Chairwoman Hartzler, Ranking Member Moulton, Subcommittee Members:

Thank you for inviting Department witnesses to testify here today, and thank you for your steadfast support for the men and women of the Department of Defense–military and civilian alike–who serve and defend our country all over the world.

Our focus this afternoon will be on Iraq, and we are pleased to discuss the Department of Defense's efforts to enable Iraq to achieve and maintain stability following the recent liberation of Mosul. The Iraqi Security Forces led the way in defeating ISIS in Mosul, liberating that city and freeing its people. The Iraqi Security Forces carried their winning momentum to the next ISIS stronghold in Tal Afar, delivering a swift victory there. One year ago, virtually all of Ninewa Governorate was controlled by ISIS. In late August, Baghdad announced the complete liberation of Ninewa Governorate. Every day, Iraqi Security Forces fight to return their country to the Iraqi people, and out of the hands of ISIS terrorists. As Iraqi Security Forces maintain the initiative and continue to bring the fight to ISIS, they are backed by strong Iraqi leadership in Baghdad and unwavering support from a 73-member global Coalition.

Although we are pleased that ISIS's military defeat is within sight, we recognize that the military effort is only one part of the Defeat ISIS campaign. The key to preventing the re-emergence in Iraq of ISIS, or any other violent extremist organization, is effective and inclusive governance. For this to develop, the United States and our Coalition partners must continue to work by, with, and through the Government of Iraq to consolidate military gains and stabilize liberated areas. This approach places the military instrument of power in a supporting and enabling role. To empower the possibility for long-term peace in Iraq, the United States and our Coalition partners are bolstering the Government of Iraq, enabling their security services, and promoting local reconciliation amongst the Iraqi people. In the fight to defeat ISIS, we saw unprecedented cooperation between the Kurdish Peshmerga forces and the Iraqi Security Forces – fighting and taking casualties to achieve a common goal for Iraq. The recent Kurdish referendum on independence presents a challenge to this cooperation, but hopefully this can be overcome.

The military defeat of ISIS is only the first step in a long-term commitment to rid the world of violent extremist organizations. The seeds of the next extremist resurgence lie in the rubble of the Defeat ISIS campaign. Following the defeat of ISIS's physical caliphate, it is vital that the Government of Iraq, with the support of the USG and the international community, continues to prioritize humanitarian assistance and stabilization efforts in order to allow the expedient return of internally displaced persons. While millions of Iraqis have returned home, over 3.2 million remain displaced as a result of the ISIS occupation.

We are working closely with the Department of State, the United States Agency for International Development, the United Nations, and our Coalition partners on near-term stabilization activities to support the Government of Iraq. Some examples of U.S. supported activities include demining, rubble removal, and restoring essential services and access to potable water. Although DoD does not possess the authority to conduct stabilization activities on its own, we continue to support our interagency partners in their efforts to stabilize Iraq, and the results speak for themselves. Over 2.2 million Iraqis, including more than a quarter million Mosul residents, have returned home. As significant as this accomplishment is, there is more work to do with our Iraqi partners. Part of ISIS's success is derived from its ability to capitalize on sectarian grievances and disenfranchisement. Allegations of abuses, extrajudicial killings, and other Law of Armed Conflict violations feed ISIS's narrative that the Government of Iraq is illegitimate. For this reason, we continue to advise the Government of Iraq on the importance of transparency and investigating all credible allegations of abuse. Prime Minister Abadi is personally committed to this effort, and has stated that he will thoroughly investigate any such allegations and hold those deemed responsible accountable in accordance with due process and Iraqi law.

Upon the physical destruction of ISIS's caliphate, we will continue the global campaign to defeat ISIS. This effort will bolster long-term stability within Iraq by engaging ISIS globally and preventing the flow of foreign fighters back to the region. The whole-of-government global campaign will continue to attack ISIS and its affiliates to further degrade their ability to recruit and maintain a fighting force. We will also continue, alongside our Coalition and interagency partners, to pressure the international community to counter the radical salafi jihadist ideology that fuels many of the world's violent extremist organizations. All of these efforts will serve to help prevent a resurgence of ISIS, provide an opportunity for inclusive and effective governance at all levels to thrive, and promote long-term stability.

Again, thank you for having us here today, we look forward to your questions.

Mark J. Swayne
Acting Deputy Assistant Secretary for Stability and Humanitarian Affairs (SHA)

Mark Swayne is the Acting Deputy Assistant Secretary for Stability and Humanitarian Affairs (SHA) within ASD for Special Operations/Low- Intensity Conflict (SO/LIC) in the Office of the Under Secretary of Defense (OUSD) for Policy. SHA develops defense policy for embassy security, humanitarian assistance, disaster response, peacekeeping, stability operations, international rule of law, prevention of atrocities, human rights, lethal autonomous weapons systems, and women, peace and security.

Mark previously served as the Director for North-West-Central Africa and Horn of Africa Regional Director in OUSD Policy. Mark retired from the U.S. Navy in 2008, and he has been working defense policy issues since January 2002. Previous to working at OSD Policy, Mark was the State Department and Interagency Liaison officer for the U.S. Africa Command's Pentagon Office.

His active duty defense policy assignments included:
- Special Assistant to the Commander, U.S. Africa Command in Stuttgart, Germany;
- Deputy POLAD for Africa, U.S. European Command;
- Director for African Affairs, White House National Security Council;
- Central and West Africa Branch Chief, Joint Staff J5 Africa; and
- Congressional Fellow to Senator John Warner.

Previous to working on defense policy issues, Mark's Naval Flight Officer assignments included:
- Admiral's Aide, Commander U.S. Second Fleet; and
- Radar Intercept Officer, F-14 Tomcat and Bombardier-Navigator, A-6 Intruder with 2,500 flying hours, 650 carrier traps, 4 aircraft carrier deployments flying over Iraq, Bosnia, and Somalia, and he led combat missions over Iraq.

Mark was commissioned through Naval ROTC at Norwich University with a B.S. in Mechanical Engineering and he has a Master of Business Administration. He and his wife Veronica have been married for 28 years and have two sons in college.

Brigadier General James W. Bierman Jr.
Deputy Director
Political-Military Affairs Middle East, J5

Brigadier General James W. Bierman, Jr. was born in Camp Lejeune, and attended the Virginia Military Institute. Upon completion of The Basic School and Infantry Officer's Course in 1988, he reported to the 2d Marine Division and was assigned as a Rifle Platoon Commander in Marine Air Ground Task Force (MAGTF) 4-88. While in this billet he participated in contingency operations in the Persian Gulf.

In December 1988, Brigadier General Bierman was assigned to 2d Battalion, 8th Marines. While with 2/8 he served as an Anti-Armor Platoon Commander, Adjutant, and Commanding Officer of Headquarters and Service Company. In 1991 he deployed to the Mediterranean with the 24th Marine Expeditionary Unit, and participated in operations in Northern Iraq as part of Operation Provide Comfort.

In February 1992, he began a tour in the Intelligence Field and was assigned to 1st Surveillance Reconnaissance and Intelligence Group for duty as an Analyst in the 1st MAGTF All Source Fusion Center. In December 1992, Brigadier General Bierman was attached to the 1st Marine Division for duty as an Intelligence Analyst in Mogadishu, Somalia during Operation Restore Hope. In May 1993 he assumed duties as the Intelligence Officer for the 1st Marine Regiment.

In June 1995, Brigadier General Bierman returned to Quantico to attend the Amphibious Warfare School. After graduating, he returned to Camp Pendleton where he served as the Commanding Officer of Company C and Battalion Operations Officer in 1st Battalion, 1st Marine Regiment. During this tour he participated in contingency operations ashore in the Central Command Area of Operations with the 13th Marine Expeditionary Unit.

From July 1999 to June 2002, Brigadier General Bierman served as the Commanding Officer of Recruiting Station Richmond, Virginia. Following recruiting duty, he attended the School of Advanced Warfighting in Quantico. While a student there he was assigned to I Marine Expeditionary Force, and participated in Operation Iraqi Freedom as a planner.

After graduating from the School of Advanced Warfighting, Brigadier General Bierman returned to I Marine Expeditionary Force. In the summer of 2003, he deployed to Al Hillah, Iraq where he served as an Action Officer during Phase IV of Operation Iraqi Freedom. In the spring of 2004, he deployed to Fallujah, Iraq where he served as the Deputy G-3, Future Operations Officer during Operation Iraqi Freedom II.

In July 2005, he assumed command of 1st Battalion, 3d Marine Regiment. During the winter of 2006, he deployed with the battalion to eastern Afghanistan during Operation Enduring Freedom VI-VII. In the spring of 2007, he deployed with the battalion to Haditha, Iraq during Operation Iraqi Freedom 06-08.1.

He relinquished command of 1st Battalion, 3d Marines in November 2007. Shortly thereafter he reported to the College of Naval Warfare in Newport, Rhode Island. In April 2009, he assumed the responsibilities as Commanding Officer, 3d Marine Regiment Remain Behind Element. In November of 2009, Brigadier General Bierman assumed command of the 3d Marine Regiment, a billet he held until of May of 2011.

From 2011 to 2013, he was assigned as the Military Secretary to the Commandant of the Marine Corps.

In July 2013, Brigadier General Bierman assumed command of Marine Corps Recruit Depot, San Diego and the Western Recruiting Region, a billet he held until 15 July 2016.

On 1 September 2016, he assumed his current duties as the Deputy Director for Political-Military Affairs for the Middle East, Strategic Plans and Policy Direction (J5), on the Joint Staff.

Brigadier General Bierman's personal decorations include the Legion of Merit with gold star, the Bronze Star with combat distinguishing device and two gold stars, the Meritorious Service Medal with two gold stars, the Navy and Marine Corps Commendation Medal with gold star, and the Navy and Marine Corps Achievement Medal with gold star.

Statement for the Record
Joseph Pennington
Deputy Assistant Secretary of State for Iraq

House Armed Services Committee
Oversight and Investigations Subcommittee
October 3, 2017

Chairwoman Hartzler, Ranking Member Moulton, and Subcommittee members, thank you for inviting me to testify today. The State Department recognizes that stabilizing Iraq and Syria requires more than battlefield success. In Syria, it also requires a political transition, and in areas liberated from ISIS, strengthened local governance, unfettered humanitarian assistance, and economic prosperity. In Iraq, it requires political stability and economic growth. We are working with our partners in the 73-member Global Coalition to Defeat ISIS to promote stability and prosperity in areas liberated from ISIS, so that we can cement the military gains my colleagues discussed earlier, help ensure that groups like ISIS do not re-emerge, and prevent Al-Qa'ida from filling the gap as ISIS collapses. Achieving stability and prosperity also helps blunt the appeal and influence of malign actors, like Iran. Despite challenges, we see significant progress with some of our key initiatives.

As a result of the stabilization component of our U.S.-led Coalition's efforts to defeat ISIS, more than 2.2 million Iraqis have returned home. The returns include over 280,000 who have gone back to Mosul, a city that was only recently liberated. In eastern Mosul, more than 97 percent of those displaced during the military campaign have already returned home. The numbers are similar in Tikrit, Ramadi, and Fallujah. Unfortunately, more than 3 million Iraqis remain displaced, but we will continue to work to help set conditions so that they can return home safely. We will also continue to provide support for those who remain displaced, including members of minority communities. The United States remains the largest donor to the Iraq response, providing nearly $1.7 billion in humanitarian assistance for Iraqis in Iraq and the region since 2014.

To help stabilize areas liberated from ISIS, the United States has contributed $115 million through USAID to the United Nations Development Program's (UNDP) Funding Facility for Stabilization (FFS), and in July announced an additional $150 million. Nationwide, UNDP has implemented over 1,100 stabilization activities focused on restoring basic services and livelihoods in areas liberated from ISIS, including nearly 350 projects in Mosul. FFS has supported scores of projects in the Ninewa Plains and Sinjar, centers of Christian and Yezidi communities. These projects, many of which are ongoing, total $22 million in Sinjar and $34 million in the Ninewa Plains. These projects include the repair of 15,000 homes and scores of schools; 18 water and 26 electricity projects; cash grants for families to restock animals and assets; and cash-for-work projects.

Demining is critical to stabilization and returning Iraqis to their homes. Since April 2016, U.S.-funded programs have cleared over 10 million square meters of land and removed over 12,000 IEDs and other explosives.

As Secretary Tillerson has said, "As a coalition, we are not in the business of nation-building or reconstruction." We know that Iraq will need to diversify from oil, right-size its public sector, reduce corruption, and pave the way for foreign investment to promote economic development and longer-term reconstruction. U.S. businesses are ready to invest in Iraq if Baghdad makes necessary reforms to improve the business climate.

Iraqi politics have been characterized by positive, if halting, momentum since the formation of the Abadi government in 2014. The upcoming national and provincial elections scheduled for spring of 2018 provide another opportunity for Iraqis to make their voices heard.

However, Iraq is also facing a major challenge as a result of the destabilizing September 25 referendum held in the Iraqi Kurdistan Region and parts of the disputed territories. Baghdad-Erbil coordination against ISIS has continued, but the tenor of that cooperation has suffered. Prime Minister Abadi is under tremendous pressure from Iraq's parliament and hardliners to respond to Erbil's action and preserve the unity of the Iraqi state. While high-level negotiations on the future of Baghdad-Erbil relations may prove difficult in the near term, we strongly believe Baghdad-Erbil dialogue on more constrained matters, such as air transportation and border control, can begin to rebuild trust.

Although Iraq continues to suffer from ethno-sectarian divisions, it is notable this election season that Iraqi nationalists, who do not wish to see their country under the thumb of Iran or any other power, are increasingly coming to the fore. We expect to see a significant number of cross-sectarian political coalitions or alliances during the next election and the government formation process that follows. Iraq's Sunnis are increasingly engaging in the political process.

Finally, the United States supports Iraq's efforts to reintegrate into the region, and we applaud the recent opening of Iraqi border crossings with Saudi Arabia and Jordan. We will support the planned Iraq-Saudi coordination committee that offers economic and security advantages for both countries.

In Syria, although the Assad regime is not a trusted host nation partner nor is there a UN stabilization coordinator, U.S.-supported UN agencies and NGOs continue to provide critical humanitarian assistance. We have also initiated stabilization assistance activities in areas that legitimate opposition groups have liberated from ISIS that have enabled tens of thousands of Syrians to return home. We continue to encourage our allies and the international community to focus stabilization efforts on liberated areas, and to refrain from providing assistance that will shore up the Assad's regime's dictatorial control and strengthen his resistance to a political transition. I will not say more on Syria at this point, but my colleague Pam Quanrud, from the Department's Office of the Special Presidential Envoy for the Global Coalition to Defeat ISIS, is here to take any additional questions on that subject.

I want to thank the Subcommittee again for the opportunity to discuss our initiatives to cement the significant military gains made in the fight against ISIS. I welcome your questions on Iraq.

Joseph S. Pennington

Deputy Assistant Secretary for Iraq

BUREAU OF NEAR EASTERN AFFAIRS

Term of Appointment: 12/2015 to present

Joseph Pennington, a Career Member of the Senior Foreign Service, began his current assignment as Deputy Assistant Secretary for Iraq, in the Bureau of Near Eastern Affairs, in December 2015. He also served as Director of the Office of Iraq Affairs after returning from a two-year assignment (2013-15) as Consul General at the U.S. Consulate General in Erbil, in the Iraqi Kurdistan Region.

Mr. Pennington served as Deputy Chief of Mission at the U.S. Embassy in Prague, Czech Republic (2010-13) and held the same position in Yerevan, Armenia (2007-10). He worked as the U.S. Embassy Spokesman in Ankara, Turkey (2002-06), political-economic officer in Naples, Italy (2001-02), and headed the U.S. Embassy Branch Office in Mostar, Bosnia-Herzegovina (2000-01). He served as an economic officer at the U.S. Embassy in Sarajevo (1999-2000), and as political-economic officer at the U.S. Consulate in Adana, Turkey (1995-98). Mr. Pennington has also worked in the State Department's Bureau of Economic and Business Affairs and at the U.S. Embassy in Moscow.

Mr. Pennington is a graduate of the University of Maryland Baltimore County (UMBC), where he earned a B.A. in political science. He subsequently earned an M.A. from Columbia University in New York City.

Pamela G. Quanrud
Director
Global Coalition to Defeat ISIS
U.S. Department of State

Pamela Quanrud assumed her duties under Special Presidential Envoy for the Global Coalition to Defeat ISIS General John Allen (now Brett McGurk) in July 2015. In that capacity, she and her team provide guidance and overall coordination to the 73 member Global Coalition to advance this international effort.

Prior to taking up this position, Ms. Quanrud served as the Regional Energy Counselor for Africa from 2013 to 2105, advancing energy issues across both geographic and technology spectrums. From 2012 to 2013, she served as Chief of Staff to Deputy Secretary of State William J. Burns. From 2011 to 2012, she served as Principal Deputy Executive Secretary. From 2009 to 2011, Ms. Quanrud was Deputy Assistant Secretary in the Bureau of European and Eurasian Affairs. In this capacity, she oversaw bilateral relations with the 19 countries of the Nordic, Baltic, Central European and Germanic-speaking regions.

Ms. Quanrud came to the European Bureau following a tour as Deputy Chief of Mission at the U.S. Embassy in Warsaw, Poland. Prior to her assignment in Poland, Ms. Quanrud served as Economic Minister Counselor in Moscow, Russia from 2004 to 2007, which followed by a decade her first tour in Moscow. From 2001 to 2003, Ms. Quanrud was Director for European Affairs at the National Security Council, with responsibility for U.S. - EU relations. Her earlier assignments include the U.S. Mission to the UN and Embassy Bonn at the time of German unification. Ms. Quanrud brings with her an extensive background in D-ISIS CT efforts, energy, trade and finance, countries in transition, the European Union, and Eastern European and Soviet studies.

She has a Bachelor's Degree from Dartmouth College and a Master's Degree from the London School of Economics. She is married and has two children.

QUESTIONS SUBMITTED BY MEMBERS POST HEARING

OCTOBER 3, 2017

QUESTION SUBMITTED BY MR. MOULTON

Mr. MOULTON. General Bierman and DASD Swayne, in your testimony you alluded to the importance of demobilizing and reintegrating Shia militias (including but not limited to the Popular Mobilization Forces)—what role does DOD have in supporting this process and ensuring demilitarization proceeds?

Mr. SWAYNE and General BIERMAN. Securing peace in Iraq will require a coordinated and strong whole-of-government approach that works by, with, and through the Government of Iraq. This approach continues placing the U.S. military in a supporting role, including in efforts to demobilize and reintegrate Shia militias. In November 2016, Iraq's parliament passed a law that stipulates that the Popular Mobilization Forces (PMF) are an independent military institution within the Iraqi Security Forces (ISF), which will be an obstacle to dissolving the PMF. Prime Minister Haider al-Abadi supports the law and is working to consolidate PMF factions not allied directly with Iran into the ISF.

As defeat-ISIS operations succeed in liberating ISIS-held territory in Iraq, the Department of Defense's (DOD) security force assistance will shift to broader institutional efforts that ensure ISF are both effective and legitimate. U.S. building partner capacity efforts will prioritize counterterrorism, critical infrastructure protection, and border control capabilities. Civil-military operations will be a critical supporting effort for each line of effort. Working closely with the Department of State, the U.S. Agency for International Development, and international partners, DOD will support the Government of Iraq's efforts to solidify viable roles for the PMF within the ISF that are not duplicative or provocative of sectarian tensions.

———

QUESTION SUBMITTED BY MR. SUOZZI

Mr. SUOZZI. Please provide a strategy document that outlines the Department of State's long-term goals and interests in Iraq and how the Department plans to implement them.

Mr. PENNINGTON. The Department of State's 2015–2017 Integrated Country Strategy (ICS) Chief of Mission Priorities for Iraq is included below. The ICS is the formal document in which the Department of State articulates its goals and country-specific policies. We will update this document in the next planning cycle to account for this Administration's priorities, including maintaining military gains against ISIS, countering malign Iranian influence, and promoting American trade and investment ties in Iraq.

Begin 2015–2017 Iraq Integrated Country Strategy Chief of Mission Priorities:

"Over the next three to five years, the U.S.-Iraq relationship will remain a key priority for the United States, grounded in our shared Strategic Framework Agreement and impelled by our shared imperative to degrade and ultimately defeat the Islamic State of Iraq and the Levant (ISIL). We are committed to helping Iraq counter ISIL by providing U.S. military advice, assistance, and training, and by supporting inclusive governance, democratic institutions, advancing human rights protections, and improving relationships with the country's Sunni neighbors. Iraq has the potential to become one of the largest oil suppliers in the world over the next 20 years, endowed with energy resources that offer the possibility of economic self-sufficiency. It also has the potential to become an influential international actor and U.S. ally, if it can overcome the sectarian violence, political division, and corruption that have characterized the last decade.

Our immediate focus in Iraq is to degrade and ultimately defeat ISIL. Mission Iraq priorities for the next three years will be: enhancing Iraq's ability to secure and defend itself and its borders; bolstering Government of Iraq (GOI) revenues, improving financial management, and encouraging effective and equitable service delivery; providing humanitarian assistance to internally displaced persons (IDPs), refugees, and vulnerable populations; and assisting in post-conflict stabilization in areas retaken from ISIL.

Mission Iraq will also implement relevant parts of the Administration's overall regional strategy to help Iraq combat ISIL. Outreach and diplomatic efforts will sup-

(91)

port political reform, disrupt and constrain ISIL's financing, address the humanitarian crisis, and expose ISIL's true nature. We will continue to facilitate coordinated security assistance and military sales, as well as provide necessary support to Iraq to implement a comprehensive strategy to isolate ISIL from the Iraqi population and develop a longer-term plan for sustainable security. Our efforts will focus on rebuilding the Iraqi Security Forces (ISF) to take the fight to ISIL, while integrating tribal fighters. Mission Iraq will work to advance the eventual transition of these fighters and other local forces into a National Guard, as well as continue to provide targeted technical assistance to strengthen the institutional and organizational capacity of the Ministry of Defense as it regenerates Iraqi Army units. We will continue to encourage Iraqi political and security leaders to ensure that the fight against ISIL is conducted in a manner that protects civilians, minimizes the impact of the conflict on them, and adheres to the rule of law. And we will continue to engage Iraq's next generation through educational and cultural exchange and social media outreach programs that offer an alternative vision to ISIL's violent extremism.

Our engagement with the GOI will continue to be broad and intense, covering a wide range of political and economic interests. While the GOI concentrates its resources and efforts on fighting ISIL, we will encourage prudent budgetary and fiscal practices that Iraq must employ to ensure it has the ability to finance the fight against ISIL, as well as to develop crucial infrastructure and deliver services in sectors such as oil and gas, electricity, housing, education, agriculture, public works, and health care. Through targeted technical assistance, we will work with key Iraqi interlocutors to encourage and support prudent financing mechanisms and multiyear budgetary planning to foster Iraq's long-term economic stability.

Humanitarian assistance, in the context of the current crisis, remains an ongoing priority as the GOI struggles to cope with the millions of displaced persons residing in Iraq. Continued U.S. and international support in the form of humanitarian assistance and stabilization is critical to ensuring that Iraq can alleviate prolonged as well as emergency displacements. An important component of this effort is a focus on Iraq's religious and ethnic minority communities, which have been disproportionately affected by ISIL's violence.

As the ISF, working with the international coalition against ISIL, begins to push ISIL out of areas over which it exercises control, the GOI will need to be prepared to fill the potential gap in government administration and services that will be left in ISIL's wake. While the GOI's primary focus now must be to concentrate on defending territory that it holds and reconstituting its capacity to retake lost terrain, Mission Iraq will begin discussions, as appropriate, with GOI partners to conceptualize a strategy for quickly reestablishing local government, relying primarily on the efficient application of GOI assets to ensure that government institutions and activities are rapidly established, held accountable, and sustainable.

In the medium to long term, Mission Iraq will continue to encourage the development of "functional federalism," aimed at decentralizing administrative and fiscal authority from Baghdad to the provinces; promoting local governance; and ensuring Shia, Sunni, and Kurdish buy-in to Iraq's democratic institutions. We will advocate for long-term resolution of the disagreements between Baghdad and Erbil regarding oil exports and revenue management and will support Iraq's efforts to pass comprehensive hydrocarbons legislation.

Also in the medium to long term, Mission Iraq will work with the GOI to increase oil production capacity. Poor project administration, procurement capacity, limited political will and inefficient policies have led to a lack of onshore pumping and limited storage capacity threaten Iraqi oil production and exports from reaching their full potential, stifling government revenue growth. Iraq also has a tremendous opportunity to harness its significant natural gas resources, which could help the country meet its domestic electricity needs. In addition to partnering to share best practices on fossil fuel production and exports, we are engaged with the GOI on capturing gas for power generation and hydrocarbons revenue management. We will encourage the GOI to continue the reforms necessary to accede to the WTO as their implementation would create an environment more welcoming to foreign investment. These reforms would open a path to Iraq's economic diversification, allowing the country to eventually become less dependent on oil revenues as the nearly sole source of GOI income."